From the Publisher

When the opportunity to purchase Skipper Bob Publications arose in late 2007 I didn't have to think twice about what my decision would be. I have always admired Skipper Bob's work. His ability to provide cruising information in a clear, matter of fact format at a very affordable price was unmatched in the cruising publication industry. His dedication to the cruising community was unchallenged.

The series of Skipper Bob books fits in well with our Waterway Guide Products, as they serve a slightly different segment of the cruising market and present the information in a different manner. No major changes to the format for Skipper Bob books are planned.

Ted Stehle serves as editor. Among his responsibilities is the process of updating and publishing each book on an annual basis and maintaining the Skipper Bob website. Primary input for updates and changes continues to be from the active cruising community, including the Waterway Guide Cruising Editors.

Elaine Reib, the late Skipper Bob's widow, continues to serve in an advisory capacity and represents Skipper Bob at various boat shows and rendezvous.

We're excited and honored to be carrying the tradition forward and look forward to hearing from you.

Jack Dozier
Publisher

Editor Ted Stehle and first mate Audrey

Ted and Audrey Stehle began boating as sailors in the early 1970's on the Chesapeake Bay and then switched to power after retirement. In addition to extensive cruising of the Chesapeake and its tributaries, they have traveled the ICW many times, completed the Great Loop, cruised the Ohio, Tennessee and Cumberland Rivers and made many trips up and down the Tenn-Tom. In addition to serving as the editor for Skipper Bob Publications, Ted is the Director of Operations for Waterway Guide.

Guides by Skipper Bob Publications

Planning Guides –

    Cruising Comfortably On a Budget. Tips on saving thousands of dollars while living and cruising on the coastal waters of the Eastern United States. How to outfit your boat and still be comfortable. ISBN 0-9662208-7-0 **$25**

    The Great Circle Route. Cruising the Great Circle Route up the East Coast, across the Great Lakes, down the Mississippi and Tenn-Tom Waterway to the Gulf Coast, and across the Gulf Coast to Florida. How to schedule the trip. ISBN 0-9662208-4-6 **$19**

    Bahamas Bound. A planning guide to the Bahamas. Who should consider going. What type of vessel. How to outfit your vessel for the Bahamas to save money and enjoy the trip. Marina prices and contact information. ISBN 0-9662208-9-7 **$16**

Cruising Guides –

    Anchorages Along The Intracoastal Waterway. Anchorages, free docks, bridge restrictions and waterway concerns from the Hudson River to Key West including the Okeechobee Waterway and St. Johns River. ISBN 0-9662208-3-8 **$17**

    Marinas Along The Intracoastal Waterway. Fuel prices, transient slip fees, courtesy cars, long-term slip fees, do-it-yourself yards, marina facilities, monthly rates, and haul out fees from the Hudson River to Key West. ISBN 0-9662208-0-3 **$15**

    Cruising the Gulf Coast. Cruising the Gulf Coast on the Gulf Intracoastal Waterway from Brownsville, TX to Flamingo, FL. Covers the waterway, anchorages, bridge and lock restrictions, marinas, and shopping along the way. ISBN 0-9727501-4-2 **$16**

    Cruising the New York Canal System. Depth and height restrictions. Lock locations and characteristics. Places to stay at no charge with water and electric. Includes the Erie, Oswego, Cayuga-Seneca, and Champlain Canals. ISBN 0-9662208-5-4 **$13**

    Cruising the Rideau and Richelieu Canals. How to plan a cruise of the historic waterways in Canada that include the Rideau Canal, Ottawa, St Lawrence River, Montreal, Quebec, Richelieu Canal, Chambly Canal, and Lake Champlain. ISBN 0-9662208-6-2 **$13**

    Cruising the Trent-Severn Canal, Georgian Bay and North Channel. Cruising the Trent-Severn Canal including fees, services available, where to stay, etc. Includes highlights of the Georgian Bay, North Channel and northern Lake Huron. ISBN 0-9662208-8-9 **$13**

    Cruising Lake Erie. Cruising characteristics of Lake Erie and Lake St. Clair. Information for a cruise including planning, approaches to ports, anchoring overnight, dockage and visiting sites ashore. List of required charts and sources. ISBN 0-9727501-1-8 **$18**

    Cruising Lake Ontario. Information on harbors, anchorages, marinas, shopping, and local attractions. Distances to harbors with GPS coordinates at the entrance to each harbor. Includes the Thousand Islands and the Bay of Quinte. ISBN 0-9727501-0-X **$17**

    Cruising From Chicago to Mobile. Cruising the Inland River System from Chicago to Mobile, AL on Mobile Bay. Information on anchorages, free docks, marinas, bridge and lock restrictions, and navigational concerns for this route. ISBN 0-9727501-5-0 **$16**

    Cruising Lake Michigan. Information on ports and harbors, approach GPS waypoints, anchorages, Lake Michigan precautions, marinas, shopping, and local attractions. Includes Green and Grand Traverse Bays. ISBN 0-9727501-5-0 **$19**

Nautical Reading –
   Seven Miles an Hour. Witty, but to the point. This book gives the reader the basic concept of what you will go through when deciding to buy a boat and live aboard. Excellent read for anyone interested in boating. ISBN 0-9727501-6-9 **$23**

Ordering Skipper Bob Publications

AGLCA – 500 Oakbrook Lane, Summerville, SC 29485
   Phone 877-478-5667. Internet – www.greatloop.org.

Bluewater Books & Charts – 1811 Cordova Road, Fort Lauderdale, FL 33316
   Phone 800-942-2583. Internet - www.bluewaterweb.com.

Defender Industries – 42 Great Neck Road, Waterford, CT 06385
   Phone 800-628-8225. Internet – www.defender.com.

Landfall Navigation® – 151 Harvard Avenue, Stamford, CT 06902
   Phone 800-941-2219. Internet - www.landfallnavigation.com/skipperbob.html.

Maryland Nautical Sales – 1400 E. Clement St., Baltimore, MD 21230
   Phone 800-596-7245. Internet – www.mdnautical.com.

The Nautical Mind Bookstore – 249 Queen's Quay West, Toronto, Ontario, Canada M5J 2N5
   Phone 800-463-9951. Internet - www.nauticalmind.com. Select "Search".

West Marine – Select locations.

Where you can pick up Skipper Bob Publications:

FL: Black Raven Ship's Store, 111 Avenida Menendez, Ste. F, St. Augustine, FL 32084,
   Ph 877-578-5050
   City of Fort Meyers Yacht Basin, 1300 Lee Street, Ft. Meyers, FL 33901,
   Ph 239-321-7082
   First Mates Ship Store, 235 Yacht Club Drive, St Augustine, FL 32905, Ph 904-829-0184
   Halifax Harbor Marina, 450 Basin St., Daytona Beach, FL 32114, Ph 386-671-3601
   Hopkins-Carter Marine, 3300 NW 21st Street, Miami, FL 33142, Ph 800-595-9656
   Indiantown Marina, 16300 SW Famel Avenue, Indiantown, FL 34956, Ph 772-597-2455
   Legacy Harbor Marina, 2044 W. 1st Street, Fort Myers, FL 33901, Ph 239-461-0775
   Palm Coast Marina, 200 Club House Dr., Palm Coast, FL 32137, Ph 386-446-6370
   Panama City Marina, 1 Harrison Avenue, Panama City, FL 32401, Ph 850-872-7272
   Pier 17 Marine, Inc., 4619 Roosevelt Blvd., Jacksonville, FL 32210, Ph 904-387-4669
   Sailorman, 350 SE 24th Street, Fort Lauderdale, FL 33316, Ph 866-729-3760
   Titusville Municipal Marina, 451 Marina Road, Titusville, FL 32796, Ph 321-383-5600

GA: Hattie's Books, 1531 Newcastle St., Brunswick, GA 31520, Ph 912-554-8677

KY: Green Turtle Bay, 242 Jetty Drive, Grand River, KY 42045, Ph 800-498-0428

LA: **Ship to Shore Co.,** 4313 Lake Street, Lake Charles, LA 70605, Ph 337-474-0730

MD: **Maryland Nautical Sales,** 1400 E. Clement St., Baltimore, MD 21230, Ph 800-596-7245
   Spring Cove Marina, PO Box 160, Solomons, MD 20688, Ph 410-326-216

NC: **Page after Page Bookstore,** 111 South Water Street, Elizabeth City, NC, Ph 252-335-7243
   Scuttlebutt, 433 Front Street, Beaufort, NC 28516, Ph 252-728-7765

NJ: **Utsch's Marina,** 1121 Route 109, Cape May, NJ 08204, Ph 609-884-2051

NY: **Brewerton Boat Yard,** 5405 Bennett Street, Brewerton, NY 13029, Ph 315-676-3762
   Ess Kay Yards, Inc, 5307 Guy Young Road, Brewerton, NY 13029, Ph 315-676-2711
   New York Nautical, 140 West Broadway, NY, NY 10013, Ph 212-962-4522
   Rondout Yacht Basin, PO Box 257, Connelly, NY 12417, Ph 845-331-7061
   Smith Boys Marina, 280 Michigan Street, N. Tonawanda, NY 14120, Ph 716-695-3472
   St. Peter's Outfitters, 3 Basin Street, Oswego, NY 13126, Ph 315-345-6683
   Troy Town Dock and Marina, 427 River Street, Troy, NY 12180, Ph 518-272-5341
   Walter Elwood Museum, 366 W. Main Street, Amsterdam, NY 12010, Ph 518-843-5151
   Waterford Canal Center, One Tug Boat Alley, Waterford, NY 12188, Ph 518-527-5041
   Winter Harbor Marina, PO Box 630, Brewerton, NY 13029, Ph 315-676-9276

PA: **Pilothouse Nautical Books,** 1600 S Delaware Ave, Philadelphia, PA, Ph 215-336-6414

RI: **NV Charts,** 62 Thames Street, Newport, RI 02840, Ph 401-239-0349

SC: **Downtown Marina,** 1006 Bay Street, Beaufort, SC 29902, Ph 843-524-4422
   Harborwalk Books, 723 Front Street, Georgetown, SC 29440, Ph 843-546-8212
   Osprey Marina, 8400 Osprey Road, Myrtle Beach, SC 29588, Ph 843-215-5353
   Port Royal Landing Marina, 1 Landing Drive, Port Royal, SC 29935, Ph 843-525-6664
   UK-Halsey Sailmakers, 3 Lockwood Drive, Charleston, SC 29401, Ph 843-722-0823

TX: **MarineMax,** 3001 NASA Pkwy, Seabrook, TX 77586, Ph 281-326-4224

VA: **Dozier's Regatta Point,** 137 Neptune Lane, Deltaville, VA 23043, Ph 804-776-6711
   Deltaville Marina, 274 Bucks View Lane, Deltaville, VA 23043, Ph 804-776-9812
   Downtown Hampton Public Piers, 710 Settlers Landing Road, Hampton, VA 23669, Ph 757-727-1276
   Mile Marker 0, One High Street, Portsmouth, VA 23704, Ph 757-673-4816
   Nauti Nell's, 16507 General Puller Hwy, Deltaville, VA 23043, Ph 804-776-9811
   Salty Dog Discount Marine, 9557 Shore Dr., Norfolk, VA 23518, Ph 757-362-3311
   WT Brownley Co, 226 E Main Street, Norfolk, VA 23510, Ph 757-622-7589

Canada:

   McGill Maritime Services, Montreal, Quebec, Ph 514-849-1125

The Nautical Mind Bookstore – 249 Queen's Quay West, Toronto, Ontario M5J 2N5
Ph 800-463-9951

NOTE: If you are not able to locate the Skipper Bob book that you desire, contact
Skipper Bob Publications, Ph 800-233-3359, ext 1#, email orders@skipperbob.net or visit
www.skipperbob.net.

Skipper Bob is proud
to be a sponsor of

TABLE OF CONTENTS

Bahamas Bound

Chapter 1
Who Should Consider Going?

Who should consider going to the Bahamas? That is an easy question. Everyone! The collection of islands referred to as "The Bahamas" off the east coast of Florida offers a paradise replete with warm temperatures, clean clear waters, abundant beaches, friendly people, great fishing and underwater sports, and ample activities to keep even the most particular person busy and content. The only place in the Continental US that even comes close to offering what the Bahamas has available is the Florida Keys.

You can fly to the Bahamas, take a cruise ship, book passage on a freighter or take your own vessel. All four methods have one thing in common. You must cross the Gulf Stream. In this book I will not address the first three methods outlined above, rather I will concentrate on taking your own vessel. I guess I could have titled this chapter of the book, "Who Should Consider Taking Their Own Vessel Across The Gulf Stream To The Bahamas?" I thought about it, but it seems like much too long a title for a chapter.

Virtually every kind of vessel has been taken to the Bahamas. Almost routinely some people take 18-20 foot open powerboats with a single outboard engine across. Others have taken un-seaworthy houseboats, and I even know of one man that towed a floating house across and left it in Marsh Harbour, Abaco. The main factor to take into consideration when crossing to the Bahamas is the weather. If the ocean would stay dead calm you could row an open rowboat across in about 40 hours.

The easiest and most comfortable way to the Bahamas is by Cruise Ship.

Before you can determine if you should cross to the Bahamas there are several factors you must consider. What time of year is it? How long do you have before you must return? How much discomfort are you willing to endure? What is the current weather forecast?

Weather controls all of your decisions. In bad weather you don't even want to think about going across. In flat calm seas with a weather forecast for light to variable winds less than 5 knots for the next 5 days, you can take just about any boat across. Unfortunately, long periods of relatively calm days are few and far between from October to March. Periods of time when it is both safe and comfortable to cross to the Bahamas are known as "Good Weather Windows". Forecasting weather windows and what to look for are covered in detail in Chapter 4. The time of year comes into play because good weather windows are most prevalent in the early summer and very scarce in mid winter. Crossing to the Bahamas from April to September is usually easier because of the long periods of light winds. However, late summer is also the beginning of hurricane season and all trips must be planned around them.

How much time you have available also plays an important part in your decision. If you only have a week, don't plan on going to the Bahamas. In mid fall you can expect a good weather window about every week. So you could wait a week before a good weather window lets you go, then it is 2-4 days to either the Abacos or Nassau, 5 days to the Exumas. Finally you want to spend a few days there. Figure on 3-4 days at your destination and then you have to return. Not only do you have the 3-4 days travel back across the banks, but also you must now wait for a good weather window before crossing the Gulf Stream back to the states. Total 3-4 weeks. I wouldn't even consider going to the Bahamas unless I had at least a month available. This time can be dramatically shortened if you are in a fast powerboat (20-25 knots) and it is June. Now you have a good weather window every 2-3 days. The trip from Florida to the Abacos can be made in 1 day. Spend two days fishing and return to the states. It can be done 7-10 days. But for most of us, going in the early fall, you should have at least a month available or you should not plan on going.

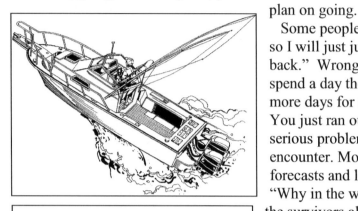

A fast sport fishing boat can make the crossing in 2-3 hours.

Some people will figure, "Well I only have a week, so I will just jump across to Bimini, and come right back." Wrong! You may wait 3-4 days to cross, and spend a day there. Then you might have to wait 3-4 more days for a good weather window to get back. You just ran out of time. This leads to the most serious problem boaters visiting the Bahamas encounter. Moving their vessel when weather forecasts and logic say they should not. When asked, "Why in the world did you go out in this weather?" the survivors almost invariably reply with something to the effect, "Well, we were on a schedule and had to be someplace by this date." You pick the date. In their heart they knew they should not be out in the weather forecast, but figured, "Oh it won't be that bad." It can be that bad and even worse! People have died because they went out in weather they should not have.

The bottom line is this. If you are planning a trip to the Bahamas, you should have a sound vessel and at least a month available to cruise. This can be shortened by half if you can break up your trip and are willing to leave your vessel in the Bahamas and return to the states by plane. Then at a later date you can fly back to the Bahamas, rendezvous with your boat and spend a little more time before returning to the states by boat. In this case, you could go with as little as 2 weeks at your disposal. However, you would be limited as to where you could go. About the only place in the Bahamas where this type of trip makes sense is the Abacos. Going to Freeport or Nassau makes no sense.They are nothing like the real Bahamas. You might as well visit Miami as visit Freeport or Nassau. Going to the Exumas is a bad idea on an abbreviated trip since there are only limited places that you can safely leave your vessel unattended for prolonged periods.

Geography

A great part of the beauty and lore of the Bahamas is the geography of the Bahamas. This same geography is what makes getting to the Bahamas difficult. If you consider the big picture, the Bahamas is a collection of more than 700 islands sitting on top of a plateau just off the east coast of Florida. Seen from the top, the Bahamas most closely resembles a flat plate under 8-10 feet of water. Around the edges of this plate are islands. On page 4 is a rough sketch of the Bahamas. The light gray shaded areas of the Little Bahama Bank and the Great Bahama Bank are generally less than 10 feet deep. Dotted around the shallow banks are islands shown in dark gray. Surrounded on all sides is the ocean with water thousands of feet deep. This unique geography provides for beautiful cruising conditions.

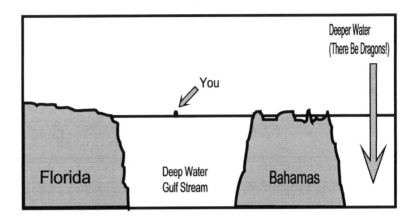

Once you have crossed the Gulf Stream and reached either of the Bahama banks, you are in relatively shallow water. And, while it is possible to have 50-foot waves on the ocean, in water 10 feet deep you cannot have 50-foot waves. So the first thing you notice when you enter the Bahama Banks is that no matter how high the waves on the ocean were when you were crossing, on the banks, they are much smaller. With a 20-knot north wind and 15-foot seas in the Gulf Stream, you might find only 3-foot waves on the banks. The main point of this is that once you reach the Bahamas, you can move with relative ease in weather conditions in which you would not try to cross the Gulf Stream.

It must be pointed out, however, that moving between the banks can also be more difficult than cruising on the banks. Note that to go from the Little Bahama Bank to the Great Bahama Bank you must cross either the Northwest or Northeast Channels. Since both of these are thousands of feet deep, you can again encounter very large waves. Also when going from Bimini to Nassau you must cross the Tongue of the Ocean, which is thousands of feet deep, and again you may experience very large waves.

One final point about the unique geography of the Bahamas. Because the area of the banks is so large, and water on them so shallow, a tremendous volume of water must enter and exit the banks with each tidal cycle. With a tide of about 3 feet and an average depth of only 6 feet on both banks

The low-lying islands close to the ocean allow the ocean waves to create marvelous beaches.

combined, nearly 50 percent of the water is flushed off the banks twice each day. This creates both good and bad results. The good result is that the flushing action keeps the waters on the Bahama banks very clear. These clear waters are exciting and provide interesting navigation problems as outlined in Chapter 5. The bad result of all this tidal action is of course the tidal currents. In some areas of the banks where a series of small islands dot the edge of the bank, the tidal water must enter and exit through a relatively narrow channel, or cut, between two islands. The tidal current at full flood or ebb can be 2-3 knots and require great care in navigation. Worse still, the unsuspecting diver that is swimming around the bank, or protected side of the island, that ventures too close to either end of the island at full ebb can easily be carried out to sea.

The final effect of this swift tide between two islands is a condition known as a "Rage". When a strong wind, and of course the waves, is coming directly at one of these narrow channels from the ocean, the outgoing tide from the bank can create large waves and confused water with very rough and dangerous conditions. Cruisers should always be wary when entering or exiting a narrow channel between two islands that leads directly to the ocean. On a day with strong winds but relatively small seas on the banks, the "Rage" can easily overcome the most competent captain and his vessel part way through the channel. Of more serious concern is those days when a distant storm is sending large waves directly at the entrance of one of these channels. Again a rage can develop even though it is relatively calm in the immediate area of the channel. Always check out the channel visually before

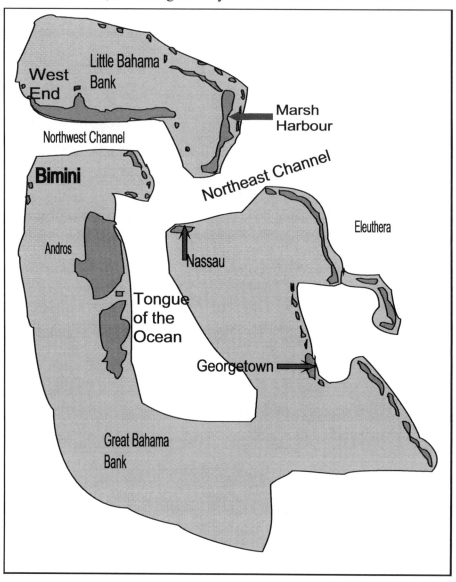

making passage and if possible ask someone who has traversed the channel recently what the conditions were like.

While cruising on the bank this tidal current, which can exceed 1 knot in the open areas, can provide problems in both navigation and swimming. From a navigational point, you can easily see the problem. If you are traveling in a straight course near the edge of one of the banks, the steady flow of current at one knot towards the edge of the bank will set your vessel off course in that direction. With the advent of GPS this does not impact cruisers today like it once did when everyone cruised by dead reckoning. You will notice from time to time, however, that if you are trying to make 90 degrees (east) that you may have to continually steer at 100 degrees to achieve a course of 90 degrees. This problem is, of course, reversed when the tide switches.

While swimming the problem can be serious. If you anchor in an open area of water about 6 feet deep and decide to take a swim, you may be shocked to discover that as soon as you enter the water you are carried away from your vessel by a relentless tide. Depending on how strong

the tide is or how good a swimmer you are this could be a fatal problem. It is recommended that before you jump in the water and go swimming on a beautiful clear day, that you wait until your vessel is securely anchored and watch how the boat hangs on the anchor line. If in doubt, tie a piece of string to a float, life cushion, or some other object and drop it straight overboard. If it is carried swiftly away from your vessel, it may not be safe to swim there. You can tie a line to each swimmer so that they can judge the effect of the water before going off and swimming on their own. However, and this is very important, keep in mind that you may have anchored

A rage can occur even though there are no strong winds in your immediate area.

at slack tide and only after you have been swimming for awhile will the tidal current pick up and start to carry you away from the vessel.

One final point about tides in the Bahamas. Since the area of the banks is so large and so much water must move off and onto the banks in a very narrow layer, the difference between high tide at one point and another on the same bank is substantial. While it may be high tide at West End on the western end of the Grand Bahama Island, it is only half tide and rising at the northern end of the Grand Lucayan Waterway 40 miles east on the north shore of the Grand Bahama Island. The tide there lags the tide at West End by almost 3 hours.

History

A quick review of the history of the Bahamas will help you get a better understanding of the people and conditions you will discover there. The Bahamas were discovered in 1492 by none other than Christopher Columbus. He landed at San Salvador, located at the southeast edge of the Great Bahama Bank. Of course, while Columbus may have "discovered" the Bahamas, it was already inhabited by a race of people called the Lucayans. Colonization being what it was, it did not take the Spanish long to kill off and enslave all Lucayans. The slaves were mostly taken to Cuba where they were worked to death. By 1600 there were no Lucayans left.

Over the next 150 years the Bahamian Islands were mostly uninhabited and largely ignored. Water routes to the Bahamas were dangerous. With the Gulf Stream and tidal current to contend with, at a time when navigation equipment was at a minimum, getting a large ship near an island was not easy. Many vessels met their end against a Bahamian Reef. Once there, there was little to keep anyone. No mineral deposits, no farmland, little if any fresh water, and a rugged terrain. The Bahamas eventually became British property and were granted to Sir Robert Heath in 1629.

The first organized group to try to settle the Bahamas was led by Captain William Sayle. Seeking religious and personal freedom, his band of about 70 tried to land in 1648 on the northeast coast of Eleuthera and were shipwrecked. Most of their provisions were lost and over the coming years the group struggled to survive in a very hostile environment. Little local fruit, almost no game and soil that begrudgingly grew meager crops meant life was hard. They survived, but never flourished. Even today, a living can be earned in Eleuthera from the land and the sea, but it requires a lot of effort.

Over the coming years numerous groups would try to settle the Bahamas with great ideas of success and riches. All would fail. The land would provide a place to live and a refuge from the sea. But only fishing and tourism would keep the Bahamians alive. Pirates chose the Bahamas for refuge and a place for a base of operations. After 100 years they were hunted down and eradicated. Wrecking would become a profession as more and more ships plied the oceans and came to an unexpected death on an uncharted reef. The locals would collect all the material off the wrecked ship and sell it or use it to buy goods to augment their life.

Columbus arrives in the Bahamas in 1492.

The American Revolutionary War caused a large influx of settlers in the Bahamas. Those American Colonists that chose to remain loyal to England during the war were treated harshly after the war. (They were called Loyalists) Many fled persecution in the new country of the United States of America and went elsewhere. Some to Bermuda, others back to England, but almost 4,000 settled in the Bahamas. They started cotton plantations (eventually killed off by a worm), salt ponds (could not remain competitive to modern mining methods), farming (land would not support long term crop growth), etc. This English ancestry is clearly visible today in the many small towns and villages throughout the Bahamas. Even more obvious are the many failed ventures. You will undoubtedly see the remains of plantations, resorts and other ventures that have been tried throughout the years.

During the period of 1780 to 1805, the last group of Bahamians to enter the stage emerged. They were the slaves. Before the Loyalists fled to the Bahamas there were probably not more than 1000 slaves in the Bahamas. The Loyalists brought an estimated 4,000 slaves with them. Over the coming years thousands of additional slaves were imported to the Bahamas. However, slavery was abolished in 1833 and the slaves became citizens of the Bahamas. Years of hard work followed, but the black population in the Bahamas has been largely absorbed into the mainstream. With interracial marriage a common occurrence, racism has been virtually eliminated in the Bahamas.

Over the years the Bahamas was to endure pirates, liquor smuggling and drug smuggling. Each flourished until the authorities could bring them under control. Because of this history, the Bahamas often gets a bad rap as a "dangerous" place to visit on a boat. The truth is that there is very little danger for the average cruiser from pirates or other criminals in the Bahamas. True, there is the occasional incident. However, no more than you would encounter along the coast of Florida. The Bahamian Government works hard to enforce the law, and while there you will probably feel a lot safer than just about anywhere on the East Coast of the US. I can tell you I feel as safe walking down a dark street in Marsh Harbour, Abaco at midnight as anywhere in the world at high noon. That being said, I would exclude the area around Freeport and Nassau as being crime free. Unfortunately these two large cities have all the crime and drug problems you might expect to find in any large city like Miami. But, when in the outlying islands, crime and drugs are not generally an issue.

By 1973, when the Bahamas was granted independence from Britain, the Bahamas had transformed itself from a deserted group of islands to a functioning nation with industry, a government, and very valuable assets; its geography and climate. Today this independent nation plays host to thousands of cruisers each year. The laws governing your visit are very lax and

encourage the boater to come. The warm climates, beautiful beaches and friendly people ensure that you will have a great time while there. So if you are asking the question, "Should we take our boat to the Bahamas?" the answer depends on whether you have a seaworthy boat, at least a month available, are willing to wait when the weather is bad, and a desire to enjoy yourself in this beautiful island country. For myself, I can't wait to get back to my winter home.

If you want to read more of the history of the Bahamas, get a copy of the book, *The Story of The Bahamas,* by Paul Albury. (ISBN 0-333-17132-2). This book is available in most bookstores in the Bahamas or can be ordered on line or from almost any bookstore in the US.

Collecting seashells is a favorite pastime of those visiting the Bahamas. The beaches are often covered with them after a storm.

The primary purpose of *this* book is to assist you in deciding if you can go to the Bahamas, assist you in planning your trip if you choose to go, and finally give you an idea of what you might find once you get there. It is not intended to replace any of the recommended cruising guides or chart kits.

Reader's comments, suggestions and recommendations are encouraged. Please feel free to write Skipper Bob Publications, PO Box 1125, Deltaville, VA 23043 or e-mail skipperbob@skipperbob.net. Contributors to this book are listed in Appendix G.

Chapter 2
Destinations

After carefully reading Chapter 1, you decide you can and want to go to the Bahamas. Where and Why?

There are a number of reasons people go to the Bahamas. Some go just to fish. They usually operate fast sport fish boats and go over to spend a week or so at one of the popular fishing marinas in Freeport, Marsh Harbour, Chub Cay (pronounced Key), or Nassau. Others are on vacation and have a couple of weeks and decide to go just to see what is there. The people I am concerned with are those cruisers that are willing to go for a month or more and are going for one reason. They want to find a place to spend the winter in warmth while experiencing a unique cruising environment.

For years we cruised south to escape the cold of the northern areas. One thing we quickly discovered was that cold fronts and cold air comes all the way south to Florida. We have all too frequently seen temperatures below freezing as far south as Tampa on the west coast and Melbourne on the east coast. Even further south you don't have relief from the cold temperatures until you get to the Florida Keys.

The reason for this is the same reason that the Bahamas remains so pleasant even during the winter. The Florida Keys and the Bahamas are surrounded by warm water. The Gulf Stream rarely gets below 75 degrees and the rest of the Atlantic surrounding the Bahamas rarely gets below 70 degrees. A small piece of land surrounded by 70 degree water just doesn't get cold in the winter when a cold front comes through and tries to drop the temperature to freezing. Therefore anywhere you stay in the Bahamas or Florida Keys you can expect very nice daytime temperatures in the 70s and only occasionally be faced with a day in the 60s.

If you are going to the Bahamas to spend your winter in a nice warm climate, you are making a good decision and anywhere in the Bahamas will do. Some people will try to convince you that the northern Bahamas (Abacos) is much colder than the southern area of the Exumas. It is not true. The average temperature difference between the two places

Looking out to sea from this Bahama island you can clearly see the many coral heads close to shore. Further out is the reef protecting the island. This is the primary reason you cannot approach most of the islands in the Bahamas from the ocean side. First you find a safe entrance onto the bank, and then approach the island from that side.

is only one or two degrees. Some days the Abacos are warmer than the Exumas and vice versa. Temperature alone is not the reason to choose between north, south or the middle of the Bahamas.

The main factor to be considered in the Bahamas both winter and summer is the winds. In the winter the winds are generated primarily by the cold fronts. These cold fronts come down from

Canada and bring with them north winds of 20-25 knots. They occur all over the Bahamas. In the summer the main wind problem is the hurricanes. They also can impact any area in the Bahamas.

As the winter goes on, the frequency of cold fronts increases throughout the Bahamas. From almost none in early October, they come through every 3-4 days by January. Then as winter goes on and spring approaches the frequency again drops off to almost none in April. The hurricane season starts in June and ends in December. However, for all practical purposes most hurricanes occur between July and September. Actually some of the best cruising can be done in the Bahamas during May and June. However, this is usually too late in the season for those planning on going north during the summer.

For most cruisers this means that you can plan to move across the Gulf Stream as early as mid October and remain safely in the Bahamas until mid June. In reality, most cruisers return in early April so that they can begin their sojourn north before temperatures along the East Coast warm up too much.

During the winter while in the Bahamas, most cruisers find themselves holed up in a safe harbor for at least 2 out of every 4 days. In between the cold fronts they can go cruising for a couple of days and then have to hole up again. Once we realized this pattern we made a decision early in our visits to the Bahamas. During the months of December to February, whether we were in the Bahamas or Florida Keys, we wanted to remain pretty much in one location. Either safely anchored in a protected harbor or in a marina. Then in between the cold fronts we could take short trips around the area where we were, but did not plan on moving any great distances because of the frequent cold fronts and strong winds associated with them.

Area I – Grand Bahama & New Providence Islands

To fit our cruising plan, we divided the Bahamas up into three distinct cruising areas; the more heavily populated and commercialized ports of Freeport and Nassau, and the lesser populated "more laid back" islands that most cruisers prefer. Area I includes includes Freeport, on Grand Bahama Island, and Nassau, on New Providence Island. Some cruisers go to the Bahamas, get as far as Freeport and spend the whole winter there, mainly in one of the upscale marinas. I should clarify that while the city of Freeport is the area in the Bahamas I am referring to, most cruisers stay in Port Lucaya, a couple of miles east of Freeport. Freeport Harbor is used primarily by large commercial vessels.

In Port Lucaya you will find gambling casinos, ready access to public transportation, ample marinas, good fishing, beautiful beaches and friendly people. The down side is that being in Freeport/Port Lucaya is very much like being in Miami and costs about the same. There is more crime than the outer islands, little if any space to anchor and you will not find many full time cruisers staying there for the winter. You won't even encounter many transient cruisers in Freeport. For the most part, cruisers visit Freeport/Port Lucaya just to see the place and then move on to the "real" Bahamas.

Nassau is very similar, but further away. There is more room to anchor in the Nassau harbor and you will see many more boats anchored there than in Port Lucaya. However, the limited marina space in Nassau is very expensive. There is a lot more transient cruiser traffic in the Nassau harbor since most cruisers going to the Exumas pass through Nassau both coming and going. Not many serious cruisers remain in Nassau for very long. It is expensive, has gambling casinos, tourist shops, beaches, friendly people and does provide a good place to re-provision However, here again it is more like Miami and, as a large city, has problems with crime.

Area II – The Abacos

Area II consists mainly of that area known as the Abacos. The Abacos offers many small islands to visit. Some have small communities on them with their quaint villages. Other islands are uninhabited and provide places where you can go to be alone and explore pristine beaches. In addition to the many great places to stay, the hub of the Abacos around Marsh Harbour offers a number of very protected harbors. Within these harbors you will find several marinas that are very reasonably priced. You can stay at a number of marinas on a daily basis for an average of $1.50/ft. There is also an upscale marina where you can spend more. Long term, a number of marinas offer facilities at $1.00/ft or less plus metered electric. Electric costs about $0.45-$0.85/KWh versus about $0.10/KWh in a U.S. marina.

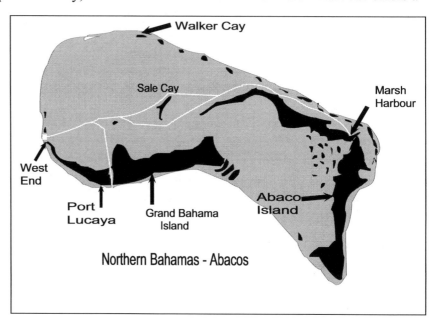

Northern Bahamas - Abacos

The Abacos with the major route shown from West End on the Grand Bahama Island to Marsh Harbour on Abaco Island. A side trip is shown south into the Grand Lucayan Canal, covered in chapter 6. To get to Marsh Harbour the cruiser goes to West End on the Grand Bahama Island and then travels in an arc across the northern part of the Little Bahama Bank finally reaching Marsh Harbour in the eastern center of the Abaco Island.

A cruiser can stay long term in Marsh Harbour at a marina for about ½ of what you would pay for a marina in the Florida Keys. Long term (90 days or longer) rates at the Marsh Harbour Marina are $0.55/ft/day. Metered electric will run $0.65/KWh and water is $50 monthly. Rates were in effect November 2012.

Marsh Harbour offers the cruiser an opportunity to stay in a marina for the entire winter at a very reasonable rate. Centrally located, when the weather is nice there are numerous communities where you can take your vessel for a day or two and then return to the safety of your marina slip when the next cold front comes through. Access to well stocked grocery stores, hardware stores, restaurants, gift shops and an airport make this area ideal for those that want to see the Bahamas without staying "on the hook" all winter.

There is ample space in the numerous harbors where you can anchor and many cruisers spend the better part of their winter there doing just that. The Abacos provides the cruiser with a place to go where you can see the Bahamas, yet be in relative comfort. Only a short sail away are many islands where you can go and be alone if you want, or anchor in the company of several cruisers. Many of those that I know that do anchor, follow a simple routine during the winter. They anchor in one of the protected harbors during the passing of cold fronts and then go to one of the many available destinations when the weather is nice. That includes, but is not limited to: Green Turtle Cay, Treasure Cay, Great Guana Cay, Man-O-War, Hope Town, or Little Harbour.

It is estimated that about 500 cruisers travel to the Abacos each winter. Most go over in November and early December. Most return to the states in April or May. At the peak, you can see as many as 100 boats at anchor in Marsh Harbour. During the past few years of the recession boat traffic to the islands was reportedly off by as much as 20%. Conditions seem to be improving, however, marinas still offer incentives.

Area III – Exuma

The third cruising destination of choice is the area known as the Exumas. The Exumas offers many small islands to visit. Some have small communities on them with their quaint villages.

Other islands are uninhabited and provide places where you can go to be alone and explore pristine beaches. The Exumas are reputed to have the most beautiful islands in the Bahamas.

Southeast of Nassau, this area provides a more remote and pristine atmosphere than the Abacos. Georgetown in the Exumas is the ultimate destination for most cruisers. While the journey to Georgetown provides for an interesting variety, most cruisers spend most of the winter anchored in Georgetown harbor.

The Georgetown harbor is quite large at nearly 1 mile across and more than 5 miles long. Because of this, when there is a significant wind shift most cruisers tend to move their

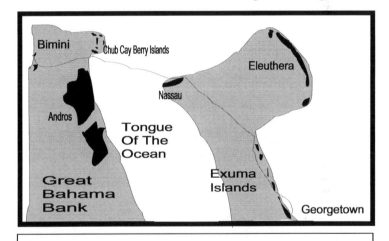

The trip to Georgetown starts at Bimini or Cat Cay and takes the cruiser across the Great Bahama Bank to Chub Cay. From Chub Cay across the Tongue of the Ocean to Nassau. Finally from Nassau down the Exuma Islands to Georgetown. Georgetown is the Mecca for cruisers in the Exumas and often hosts nearly 500 vessels at the peak in the winter.

vessel for greater protection. As fronts come through on a regular basis this means cruisers spend a lot of time jockeying for position in the crowded harbor.

There is only one marina where you can stay in Georgetown, Master Harbour Marina (formerly George Town Marina).

There are a couple of really protected anchorages, such as Hole #2, however they will only handle 8-10 boats. With several hundred boats there at one time, those that do go to Georgetown must plan on anchoring out in relatively open water.

The harbor at Georgetown is quite large and because of this, in strong winds just getting to town from the opposite side of the harbor in your dinghy can be difficult if not impossible. It is here where an inflatable dinghy with a good size motor is almost a must. The community does offer an airport, well-stocked grocery, hardware, banks, etc.

The boating community is very close knit in Georgetown. Daily activities are organized on the different outlying beaches and islands. For this reason, most boaters go to Georgetown for the activities shared with fellow boaters. There are no other communities within easy access from Georgetown. Thus, cruisers do not tend to go there to take numerous side trips during good weather. Those that stay in Georgetown tend to immerse themselves in the cruiser activities or go stir crazy.

Most cruisers arrive in December and stay until March and the "Cruisers Regatta". The Georgetown Cruisers Regatta is a very popular event with races, parties and all the excitement of the biggest race in the Bahamas.

Other Destinations

Once you start looking at charts of the Bahamas you will find other areas that I have not mentioned. Three notable areas are Eleuthera, Andros, and the Berry Islands. Andros is the largest Island in the Bahamas and the least hospitable. Approaches are fraught with reefs and there are no significant settlements or harbors. Most first time visitors to the Bahamas do not go to Andros and few of those making repeated trips to the Bahamas venture that way.

Eleuthera offers a pleasant stops for cruisers who come "the northern route" through Marsh Harbour down to Eleuthera and then on to the Exumas. The small town of Spanish Wells is friendly and clean. The Berry Islands are a

Anytime you find a good Class A harbor, expect it to be busy and usually full.

delightful group of islands midway between Bimini and Nassau. Most cruisers bypass these islands in their rush to get on to Nassau and the Exumas in good weather. Reluctantly I have to agree. If you are headed for Georgetown you want to keep moving when you can and get to the Exumas while the weather is good. If time permits you might want to spend a week or so in the Berry Islands during your return to the states in the spring when the weather is more settled.

Marinas

One important factor in going to the Bahamas is the cost of staying in marinas. Appendix D and E provides a list of nearly all the marinas in the three cruising areas covered with transient and monthly fees. Review this list if part of, or most of your time in the Bahamas will be spent in marinas. It is important to note that the marinas will often offer better rates for a longer commitment; like 3 months. A further discount may be had by offering to pay by cash (not credit card) and/or paying the entire period up front. Ask; you may be pleasantly surprised.

Finally, Appendix F provides contact information, the number of slips, the distance in miles to the nearest community or town, and some of the amenities for these same marinas. You can check on the availability of space in any marina during the time period when you plan to be there, and possibly make a reservation. Regarding reservations, a few qualifying comments are in order. Reservations are frequently changed due to weather, breakdowns, schedule changes, etc. It is estimated that only 50% of the cruisers who make reservations show up on the original date, although most reschedule. In addition, it is not uncommon for transients to extend their stay, thus causing a potential shortage of slips. Never the less, you will find that most marinas prefer and accept reservations.

Summary

If you are going to the Bahamas for the winter to enjoy great weather and beautiful beaches you probably want to consider either the Abacos or the Exumas as your final destination. The

trip to the Abacos is easier than the one to the Exumas. The Abacos is closer so the trip is shorter, and once across the Gulf Stream you have no more deepwater (>50') passages until you arrive in Marsh Harbour. The trip to Georgetown is longer and requires a second deep water passage. There are no open water overnight passages in route to the Abacos. En route to Georgetown you must plan an overnight trip from the area of Bimini to Chub Cay.

En route to the Abacos you can stop at Port Lucaya and experience the big city life, gambling casinos, and tourist shops. En route to Georgetown there is Nassau with the same amenities.

Once there, the Abacos offers greater protection, more variety and many inexpensive marinas if you want to stay in

A long wooden dock extending out into the shallow waters off the small fishing community of Cherokee in the Abacos.

a marina. Georgetown offers more pristine conditions and more organized activities with fellow cruisers, but not much in the way of marinas. Both offer close ties with a Cruisers Net (VHF-68 – see chapter 5).

The Abacos caters to both sailboats and trawlers and includes those that wish to anchor and those that want to stay in a marina. The Exumas is populated primarily by sailboats and virtually everyone anchors out. A couple of new class A marinas have been constructed in the Exumas.

The biggest complaint I have heard about the Abacos is that it is becoming too civilized. It is loosing its flavor of an out island Bahamian community. The biggest complaint I have heard about Georgetown is having to stay at anchor for days on end in strong winds with the boat rocking and rolling.

For the first time visitor to the Bahamas I strongly recommend you consider the Abacos first. They are easier to get to and provide better protection in route. Once there the support system is better and you can work all the bugs out of your vessel before trying more remote areas. If you choose to visit the Exumas you can just as easily go on from the Abacos and spend a month or more visiting the Exumas. From my standpoint visiting the Exumas in May is ideal. The winds are far less and the area less crowded. I don't think I could be happy at anchor in one harbor for the better part of 3-4 months; I don't care what activities you organize on shore.

Chapter 3
Outfitting

Once you have decided to go to the Bahamas you need to start outfitting your vessel almost immediately. The reality is that you could go to the Bahamas without taking much of anything except money and get along quite well. The downside is that it might cost you two or three times as much to do it that way.

In the Bahamas there is no income tax, capital gains tax, purchase or sales tax, Value Added Tax (VAT) or capital transfer tax. There is a stamp duty on property and mortgage transactions and a tax on real property. Businesses also pay a stamp duty on capital. As a result, most government revenue is derived from duties on imports. These duties, which are levied on the CIF (cost, insurance, freight) value, range from 0% to 150% or more. The average is around 35%. In addition, the economy is service based, with very little manufacturing or farming.

As a result, everything is more expensive in the Bahamas. It is therefore wise to provision properly prior to departing the United States. Since there are no import duties or restrictions as to what you may take to the Bahamas aboard your vessel significant cost savings may be achieved.

Cruising Permit

The policy for vessels clearing into the Bahamas (as of November 2012) is as follows: A pleasure vessel with 4 persons or fewer arriving in the Bahamas shall be subject to a fee of $150 for boats under 35' and $300 for boats over 35'. **Note:** During 2012 Customs changed the vessel size was changed to 30' but in a short period of time reversed itself and reinstated the 35' qualification. This covers the cost of an initial-entry cruising permit, plus a return visit within ninety (90) days; a vessel would be exempted from additional fees within that 90-day period, except for transportation fees if officers have to come to your boat, such as in Nassau. This also covers a three-month fishing permit and any attendant fees payable to a Customs Officer, as well as any overtime and travel costs required for the attendance of an Immigration Officer, plus the $15 departure tax should you need to fly home. (Bring a copy of your cruising permit to the airport.) Each additional person over four will be charged $15. No charge for children under 6 years old. There should be no overtime, holiday, or transportation charges above this fee. Ask for a receipt, get the name of the officer, and call Customs (242-326-4401 or 325-6551) or Immigration (242-322-8504/7530-39) in Nassau if you have any problems. You may want to call Customs before you cross the Gulf Stream into the Bahamas to verify fees. POLICY CAN CHANGE.

Customs Decal

When you return to the US with your vessel you are required to have a US Customs decal. (Vessels over 30' only!) I know that it seems silly to worry about this now, when you are just planning on leaving, but it is so much easier to have the decal on board when you return than to struggle with getting one when you return. You may apply for the decal on line by visiting https://dtops.cbp.dhs.gov. The fee is currently $27.50 for the calendar year (November 2012).

Now for the tricky part. If you are going to the Bahamas in the fall and plan to return in the spring, you must buy the decal for the year you want to return so that the decal will be valid that year. I had found out that if I filled out the form and sent in my check about January 2nd each year, it would be returned to my permanent mailing address by mid January. While in the

Bahamas, I had my mail forwarded once per week and it took about 10 days to reach me. Thus, by the end of January I would have my decal for that year. If you don't have your decal when you return you will probably be asked to find a way to the local customs office to buy one.

So at this point, it is a good idea to obtain a copy of the customs decal form immediately. If you are going to the Bahamas and returning this year, get the decal now. If you are going over this year, but plan to return next year, specify next year for the date you want on the decal.

Customs & Border Patrol
Passport Requirements & "Local Boater Option" Program

When returning to the U.S. you must present a Passport, Passport Card, or other approved documents. For cruisers returning to Florida from foreign waters a voluntary program allows eligible cruisers to register themselves and their vessels with CBP. Once registered, the program may provide expedited customs and immigration clearance through a single phone call in lieu of a port-of-entry face-to-face inspection. You are encouraged to visit www.cbp.gov for more details. Click on Travel, and then U.S. Citizens for entry documents. Click on Pleasure Boats and Aircraft, then Pleasure Boat Reporting Requirements for information on the "LBO" Program.

Pets

Pets are permitted in the Bahamas and can be taken in aboard your vessel, however, some advanced planning must be done. An import permit is required for all animals. Applications must be made in writing to the Director of Agriculture, Ministry of Agriculture, Trade and Industry, PO Box N-3704, Nassau, The Bahamas. For information call 242-325-7413/7502. The application must be accompanied by a $10.00 processing fee for each animal and a $5.00 fax fee if you wish to have the permit faxed to you. Payment should be international money order or postal order. Personal checks are not accepted and do not send cash. Allow up to two months for processing. You can print a copy of the application by visiting www.bahamas.com and searching for "pets".

Pets must have a permit

The following are the main provisions of the import permit as it applies to dogs and cats:

 a. The animal must be 6 months of age or older.
 b. The animal must be accompanied by a valid certificate which substantiates that it has been vaccinated against rabies within not less than one months and not more than ten months prior to importation for a one year vaccine. For a three year vaccine it must be no less than one month and no more than thirty-four months.
 c. The animal must be accompanied by a Veterinary Health Certificate presented within 48 hours of arrival in the Commonwealth of The Bahamas to a licensed veterinarian for examination.

Courtesy Flag

While sailing in foreign waters, you are expected to display the courtesy flag of that country as well as the flag of your own country. You can purchase both the courtesy flag for the Bahamas and the yellow quarantine flag at a local marine store or on-line for about $20 each. When arriving in Bahamian waters, raise the quarantine flag to the top of your starboard spreader. Leave this yellow quarantine flag up until after you clear customs. Only the captain should leave the vessel until you clear customs and you should not remove anything from your vessel until after you have cleared customs. Not even trash! Once you have cleared customs, lower the quarantine flag and raise the Bahamian courtesy flag. In lieu of a starboard spreader, the flags can be displayed on a short flagstaff on the bow.

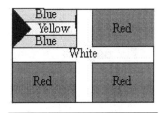

Courtesy Flag

Yellow Color

Quarantine Flag

Safety Equipment

Although flares are required at all times on vessels over 26 feet long, now is a good time to make sure you have not only the required flares, but extra ones as well as a few parachute flares. It is doubtful that you will ever need them, but if you do, you won't have time to go out and buy them. Along with flares you should make sure you have all the required safety equipment on board. This includes whistle, horn, mirror, offshore life jackets, etc. A life raft and EPIRB should also be considered. Not only should you have this equipment for common sense safety reasons, but there is also a higher than normal possibility that you will be boarded by the US Coast Guard when you return to US waters. There is no point in getting a citation when returning from a great trip to the Bahamas. You should get the equipment before you leave the states, because you don't want to pay for it in the Bahamas. This is also a good time to go over your vessel thoroughly. Crossing the Gulf Stream is not something to be afraid of, however, the Gulf Stream is due a lot of respect and you should make sure you are properly prepared for these waters.

Documentation

Both you and your vessel require proper documentation to enter the Bahamas. If your vessel is federally documented, you will be required to have a copy when you arrive in the Bahamas. If it is simply registered in some state, you will need a copy of the registration. **Important note:** Bahamas Customs requires that you leave a copy of the vessel's documentation or registration with the Customs officer. You would be well advised to make a copy of your original and bring it with you so you can give them the copy. You and **each of your passengers** must also be documented. Having a passport book or passport card is the recommended method. It will also expedite your return to the United States. Both documents may be obtained on line by visiting http://travel.state.gov/passport. Costs when ordered on line are $110.00 for the book and $30.00 for the card plus a $25 fee (November 2012) if it is not a renewal.

Dinghy

Your dinghy is your family car. It is how you will travel most of the time in the Bahamas. A great number of places where you stop, you will not be in a marina or be able to tie to a dock. The only practical way to shore is by dinghy. All too often, the distance from where you anchor to where you want to go ashore will be a ½ mile or more. You want a seaworthy dinghy with adequate power to get you to where you want to go safely and in a reasonable amount of time.

The most practical dinghy is a hard bottomed inflatable (RIB) with outboard. Although not the type of dinghy you can deflate, roll up and store away, you will find this type of dinghy far superior to anything else on the market. The hard dinghies are generally too unstable to be comfortable in all the sea conditions you will encounter in your dinghy and have far too small a carrying capacity. The soft bottom inflatables are generally too hard to steer in cross winds and don't do real well in this environment when beaching them.

A hard bottomed inflatable is almost a necessity for travel in the Bahamas. Add a good outboard and you have your "automobile".

Do not underpower your dinghy. Trips ashore will include grocery shopping and possibly "hauling" other items. You may at times have more than two persons aboard. In addition you will want to explore, go snorkeling, etc. Finally, you will occasionally find yourself in the dinghy when the sea conditions aren't ideal. So, have a motor with the spare horsepower that can respond to these needs.

Once you have the dinghy you are going to take to the Bahamas with you, make sure there is a way to stow it on your vessel. Do not consider towing the dinghy to or around the Bahamas. An astounding number of dinghies are lost each year because the owner towed it instead of stowed it. During the crossing of the Gulf Stream and during all passages of more than a couple of miles while in the Bahamas you should stow the dinghy securely on your vessel. I even recommend stowing the dinghy aboard overnight while at anchor. I can't tell you the number of people who have had their dinghy "stolen" at night during a bad wind when it was tied up astern of their boat. Then the next day or several days later the stolen dinghy is found sunk or blown ashore at some distant point because the dinghy painter parted or some of the hardware securing the dinghy broke. I once saw an inflatable dinghy standing straight out from the stern of an anchored sailboat about 5 feet above the water pin wheeling on the painter as the wind blew in gusts up to 50MPH. Too often we forget that while our vessel may be securely anchored in a safe harbor protected from large ocean waves, our dinghy feels the full force of these winds and being very light can and will flip over, break loose, and deposit all the contents therein into the water.

Stopping your dinghy is as important as propelling it. Be sure your dinghy has a good anchor system. A three-pound mushroom on a 10-foot line is NOT a good system. If you are traveling along and your dinghy motor quits, you may be in a place where the wind and/or current will carry your powerless dinghy out to sea. You want an anchor that will hold you securely in place until you get the motor running or assistance can come. Buy a small Danforth anchor and put 50 feet or more of line on it. Keep it in the dinghy where you can easily get it at anytime.

Make sure you have a provision to remove the dinghy motor and store it securely on your vessel, unless you can hoist the dinghy and motor aboard and secure them to your vessel as one unit. As a matter of practice always secure your dinghy on your vessel for any passage of over 2-3 miles, in any weather conditions where strong storms might come by, and overnight while at anchor. It is far easier to stow the dinghy and/or motor in the pleasant evening breeze than to have to get up at 3AM and try to rescue your dinghy and/or motor in the middle of a sudden squall. If you are going to be in the Bahamas more than a week, you will eventually experience a squall. Hopefully you will be secure in a safe harbor and you will not have to worry about saving your dinghy in addition to watching your anchor line.

For security when going ashore, lock your motor to your dinghy and also use a locking cable to secure the dinghy to the dock or other structure. You should also use the cable if you leave your dinghy in the water at night.

Finally, there will be times when you will use your dinghy will after dark. Make certain you have appropriate running lights.

Spare Parts

Before departing your vessel should be in top operating condition. Any item that is questionable should be repaired. However, we know that during any extended voyage routine maintenance will be required and it is possible to have a part or system break down. Be prepared. Have the required amount of oil and oil filters on board for planned oil changes. Have several extra fuel filters on board. You should have all the routine parts on board, including but not limited to, previously mentioned oil and fuel filters, air filters, fan belts, raw water impeller, a spare injector, zincs, o-rings, gaskets, etc. Don't bother to try to carry all the parts you "might" need. You cannot possibly guess what part may or may not break on your vessel. If you carried an entire spare motor, the motor mounts would fail and you wouldn't have them. Rather, make sure you have all the maintenance parts you normally use. You may need them.

For that unusual failure you will have to depend on one of three sources. If you are in an area where a number of cruisers are located, you can contact them by VHF radio and ask if anyone has the part you need. You will be surprised what some boaters carry on their boats and motors and generators have a lot of things in common. The "Cruisers Net" is a good source of technical help as well as parts. I cover the Cruisers Net (VHF 68) in detail in chapter 5.

Plan on performing almost all maintenance on your vessel and engine yourself.

If using the VHF radio fails, check at the closest local marine repair facility. You might get lucky and actually find the part you need locally. The part will be much more expensive than you ever thought, but they may have it. Ask other boaters via the VHF radio where a good repair facility is and whom they recommend for help. Someone always knows the best place to check locally. I once had to get in a Taxi in West End on the Grand Bahama Island and travel 35 miles to talk to the only local expert on our Volvo Diesel engine. He had the part and fixed my engine in 5 minutes once he got there (3 days later).

Your final option is to order the parts from a reputable dealer in the states. It is a good idea to find out who will ship you parts for your engine/generator before you leave the states. Get their fax number, phone number, E-mail address and street address. You cannot imagine how much harder it will be if you try to get this information while you are broken down in Georgetown, Exumas. Spare and replacements parts may be brought in duty free, however, they are subject to a 6% stamp duty on the value of the parts. This is the policy as of November 2012 and it would be wise to check with the Comptroller of Customs (242-326-4401) prior to importing parts. In addition, be prepared for a possible extended delivery time.

I once worked with a fellow cruiser in the Bahamas who had a bad transmission. He tried to get it repaired locally. The mechanic quoted him $3000 and one month. I told my friend he should sail back to the states and get it repaired there. He insisted that he was this far along and didn't want to go back to the states. He planned to go on to the Exumas. To make a long story short, the repair was completed improperly, it didn't work, $2000 more and when installed it ran backwards. He was told he had the wrong propeller installed (left hand instead of right hand). More repairs. Another $1000. Still didn't work. Finally he flew back to the states with the transmission in hand and had to replace the entire transmission since the repairman who worked on it in the Bahamas had so badly damaged it.

(Remember the commercial, "Gee boss, I always wanted to work on a transmission!"). The moral of the story is this. Get it fixed in the Bahamas if you feel comfortable about the level of work you want done. Major repairs to electronic equipment, engines and generators should be performed in the states. Repair to your sails, vessel and minor repairs to your engine or generator can usually be handled with no problem while in the Bahamas.

> Be very careful if you hire someone to work on your vessel! There are no warranties in the Bahamas.

The majority of repairs and maintenance you have performed on your vessel while in the Bahamas should be made by you or under your direct supervision. Major repairs should not be performed there. Don't make the mistake of pressuring the local mechanic into trying to fix your problem. All too often this leads to disaster when you push an inexperienced mechanic into doing something he has neither the training nor equipment to do. If you carry a well-rounded stock of normal maintenance parts you will probably do just fine. If you need something unusual, you will probably get it without a problem. Be prepared to spend time working on your own vessel and working with others on their vessel. Volunteering to help others accomplishes two things. First, you learn how to make the repairs. Second, you develop a close-knit group of friends willing to help you if you break down. When in the Bahamas, you are all in the same boat. There is closeness between cruisers in the Bahamas that you will not experience anywhere else. Ed. Note: The availability of repair services has improved over the years and many areas, including Freeport and Marsh Harbor, offer excellent repair facilities with factory trained personnel.

Anchors

While in the Bahamas, you will anchor out more than you normally do. But, more importantly, you will be anchoring in situations that can be a real problem if your anchor system fails. I will never forget my first trip to the Bahamas in 1979. We had just arrived and anchored in the protection of a small island on the edge of the bank. We anchored in a small horseshoe shaped cove with protection from the wind that was coming from the east. Unfortunately, to our

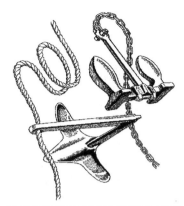

stern was the opening and the ocean only ¼ mile away. We felt safe though since winds were forecast to continue from the east for the next couple of days.

After a great day on the beach in the company of the crews from about 10 other boats anchored there, we returned to our sailboat and secured our dinghy on the deck for the night. Just before dark I noticed one of the sailboats anchored off to our port drifting. I was sure his anchor was dragging. Winds were very light so I must assume he did a really bad job of setting his hook, or perhaps the shackle came loose. In any event I wasn't the only one to notice the sailboat drifting. We sounded our horn and turned on our spotlight. No response. After some tense minutes one of the other cruisers got

A good reliable anchor system is essential for a carefree and enjoyable trip to the Bahamas.

his dinghy back in the water and was just about to set off after the drifting vessel, when a head came up in the cockpit. Needless to say, they brought their sailboat back into the protection of the cove and anchored properly for the night.

A number of us discussed the matter on the VHF. (The drifters never did answer) The point of the conversation was about what would have happened if they had improperly anchored on their own. What if there was no one there to wake them or what if it had happened after we all went to sleep. There is no doubt that they would have drifted out into the Gulf Stream and then been carried north at 3 knots. In the morning they would wake to a vessel rolling much harder than they would expect, somewhere on the ocean with no land in sight. We did not have Loran or GPS in those days, nor did anyone. Once out of the sight of land, the boater would not know what direction to head for land in the Bahamas. Unless he had a working Radio Direction Finder (RDF) as we did, he wouldn't have a clue as to what direction to head for the nearest island on the Bahama Bank. If he drifted too far north and just headed east, he would sail 3,000 miles before he ran into land. His only option would be to head west to Florida, find his location, and then head back to the Bahamas.

This positive scenario assumes a large ship did not run down the drifting vessel in the night or that a bad storm didn't come up. The bottom line is this. You must be able to anchor securely to be safe in the Bahamas. Most nights you will be anchored in a sandy bottom with varying amounts of grass. You never have to anchor in water greater than 15', so 300 feet of line will suffice. If you have rope you should consider adding at least 20' of chain next to the anchor, rather than the standard 5 or 6 feet, for chafe protection. Even though you might be anchored in sand, it will still contain pieces of coral or other material that will eventually cut through line.

No matter what kind of anchor you prefer, you should have at least two complete anchor systems. From my experience, the best anchor for the Bahamas is the Danforth and the worst is the CQR. Other than that observation, I will leave the decision as to which anchor to carry up to you. All shackles should be wired so the bolt cannot work loose. Have chafe gear available to protect the line where it enters the boat rail. If all chain, be sure to have a rope or shock system to avoid snapping your bow when the anchor chain comes taunt.

You also need a complete spare anchor system. I have seen storms damage an anchor, boats run over an anchor line and cut it, and boats cut their anchor line to get free in an emergency. Again, you don't want to be replacing your anchor system at Bahamian prices.

Finally, you should have a storm anchor system. You may be in the Exumas having a great time when a "norther" comes through. You don't want to depend on a routine anchor system to hold you in a real storm. To your stern may be rocks or open ocean. You don't want to head for either at night in a storm.

Under normal conditions, plan on putting out two anchors every night. First, you will sleep a lot better, and it does not cost you anything but time, of which you have plenty. Second, remember the strong currents in the Bahamas. They switch direction every 6 hours. You will want to learn to anchor Bahamian style with one anchor set in the direction of the current at all times.

While outfitting be sure that all your anchors, line, chain, and shackles are in good shape and of the proper size for your vessel. You will depend on them very heavily while in the Bahamas.

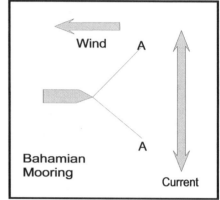

Fishing Equipment

This is an easy subject to address. If you are in to fishing, you probably already have all the rods and reels you would ever need while in the Bahamas. One rule to keep in mind; if you have more than six rods and reels on your boat, you will be classified as a commercial fishing vessel. The fee for entering the Bahamas in this case is staggering. All you really need is one good stout short rod. You can troll for fish or sit at anchor and catch all you want.

Lures are another matter. Everyone has there own preference. In fact, people catch fish in the Bahamas on just about every type of lure imaginable. Just remember this rule. "Little lure, little fish; big lure, BIG fish!" If you don't have any success with the lures you already have, ask around the area in the Bahamas where you are. There is always a store nearby where you can get the popular local lure or fresh bait.

A friend of mine cruised the Pacific in a sailboat for 12 years. After 60,000 miles he told me there was only one way to fish. He bought a number of stainless steel flat spoon type lures. To them he would attach 6 feet of stainless steel leader. At the end of the leader he attached 30 feet of clothesline. He would tie the clothesline off to the stern cleat. When he wanted to catch fish he threw the lure overboard and trailed it about 35 feet behind his boat. He would pull up about two feet of line next to his stern and attach it to the lifeline with a clothespin. Whenever he had a strike, the line would go tight, and the clothespin would pop off the lifeline alerting him to a fish. He claimed he cruised at his normal speed and caught all the fish he could eat.

Remember! Little lure, little fish; big lure, BIG fish!

In 1997 he came to the Bahamas to visit me aboard his trawler. He used the same approach for fishing. In route to Marsh Harbour, Abaco he caught 4 King Mackerel and one Grouper. He literally filled his small propane freezer with fresh fish and had to stop fishing. His comment when people complained about not catching fish was, "You just don't know what you are doing!" I have to believe him. I ate some tasty fish he caught.

Fishing Regulations

The regulations were revised in 2007 and it is recommended that you visit www.bahamas.com/bahamas/fishing to review them in detail. A few very important facts follow:

- Everyone must have a permit. (You receive one for the boat with your cruising permit).
- Bag limits are for the boat, not each individual.
- You may not use scuba gear for fishing.
- The Hawaiian Sling is the only approved spearfishing device. (You must ask to have this added to your permit).
- There is no fishing in the national sea parks.

Scuba and Snorkel Gear

If underwater sports are your thing, you are headed in the right direction. You can snorkel or scuba dive to your hearts content. Take all your gear with you. If you have not been qualified as a scuba diver, there are many places in the Bahamas where you can take lessons and be certified. At the very least, everyone on board should have a mask and flippers.

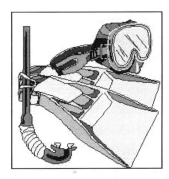

Bring your snorkel gear; you will get to use it.

Many parks and protected areas have been set aside where you can swim in water less than 15 feet deep and dive down and observe the wide variety of fish and underwater plants. In addition to this, you will want to be able to examine and clean the bottom of your boat while in the Bahamas. We find that a growth accumulates on the underwater paint about every 30 days. So once every 30 days we take our vessel into a shallow bay at low tide and drop our anchor. Then we jump in the water with swim masks and scrub pads and clean the bottom of the boat. This gets rid of the growth and "freshens" the paint. It is also a good time to check zincs. We find they need replaced about every three months in the warm waters of the Bahamas.

Be sure to stock up with all the underwater gear you may need in the Bahamas. The good news is that there is always an excellent selection of products for sale in the Bahamas and they are generally not too much more expensive than their counterpart in the states.

Satellite TV

The first few years we went to the Bahamas were rough. There was no local TV, no radio, and VHF weather broadcasts were not available. Then in 1995 we bought one of the new 18" satellite dishes. What a difference. We were able to get the Weather Channel and suddenly we knew what the weather was going to be each day. We could avoid getting caught in exposed areas as the strong winter cold fronts came through. This device was so popular, that we called it the "Abaco Flower". Today, most cruisers going to the Bahamas have satellite TV.

Marine systems are available from several manufacturers. Some track the satellite signal while travelling or at anchor, others do not. You should consider how much time you will spend at anchor and how much time you will watch TV before choosing a system. Programming is available through DirecTV or Dish Network. DirecTV also has a Bahamian operation but it is not necessary to subscribe through it. Your U.S. based subscription should work just fine, although several cruisers have reported that they lost signal when in the Exumas.

Radios

Your most valuable communication method will be the VHF radio. It is not only your ship to ship and ship to shore communication tool of choice, it is your telephone. You will find the enforcement of VHF radio protocol almost nonexistence in the Bahamas. This has come about because the Bahamians used the VHF radio literally as a phone when telephones were nonexistent or cost prohibitive. House to house calls were routine. Today, even though phones are more readily available, the VHF radio is often used by families to check on each other or just to chitchat.

Cruisers pass information on local VHF nets in the areas where many gather: Nassau, Marsh Harbour and Georgetown. One of the most popular is "The Cruisers Net" with gathers each day at 0815 on Channel 68.

With time, certain channels have been set aside for specific functions. In Marsh Harbour, as an example, channel 6 is used for communication with taxis. Refer to the cruising guide that I have recommended for a specific list of VHF channel usage in the Bahamas and try to adhere to these guidelines. In general, VHF channel 16 is for emergencies and hailing commercial enterprises. By agreement, VHF channel 68 is used for hailing cruisers. Do not use VHF channel 68 as a working channel even if you hail someone on channel 16. Switch to one of the other available working channels instead.

Remember that while the requirement to have a VHF ship station license was eliminated while in US waters, it is still required when in International waters. Therefore, you are required to have a station radio license for your VHF radio if you go to the Bahamas. If you don't have one, you can get one from the FCC. You can write to the FCC at PO Box 1050, Gettysburg, PA 17326 or call 800.418.3676 for information. You may also download the forms or file an application on line by visiting www.fcc.gov. The correct form is now the FCC Form 605 and at last check the fee for a VHF license is $200.

On your vessel you should have at least two VHF radios while in the Bahamas. There should be one at the topmost helm station and one in the main salon. You will have the radio in the main salon on almost all the time, so that you can keep in touch with all your friends and what is going on in your area. Further, a portable VHF radio is a good idea for when you go ashore with the dinghy. Often there will be times when one of you goes ashore and the other remains on the boat. The portable VHF radio allows one of you on the boat to call the other ashore and remind them to pick up a fresh loaf of bread.

A regular AM/FM radio is not much use in the Bahamas. There are a few weak stations available, but most cruisers find little of interest on them. You may be lucky and be in an area where you can receive some local weather information, but I wouldn't hold out much hope for that. In the Abacos FM 93.5 is a local station with good weather information, when it is on the air.

A Single Side Band radio allows you to reach out tremendous distances and be in touch with people all over the Bahamas as well as the US. They also allow you to check on weather, send and receive E-mail, and call home whenever you want. There are several "nets" including Cruiseheimer's Net and the Caribbean Weather Network. A ship's station license is also required for a SSB radio.

For ham radio operators, many "nets" exist including a weather net operated by the Bahamas Air Sea Rescue Association (BASRA).

For weather you may want to consider purchasing the appropriate equipment to receive Sirius Marine Weather or Wx Worx.

Water

Water is available throughout the Bahamas, and in many instances it is reverse osmosis. In marinas there will be a fee and you will pump it aboard just as you always have. In other settlements you may find it free (make a donation to the local schools/churches), or you may collect water from the local well or cistern and carry it to your boat in 5-gallon jugs. Finally you will learn to collect it as rainwater and make good use of it. In the Abacos water is available at all marinas and runs from $0.25/gal to $0.40/gal for transients. In the marinas, monthly customers may pay the per gallon rate or a flat fee of up to$60 per month. Most cruisers that limit their travels to the Abacos do not find a need or use for a water maker.

In the Exumas, water is generally harder to find and more expensive. Marina prices are about $0.50/gal for both transient and monthly stays. Some vessels decide to put a water maker on board just because of their planned travels in the Exumas. However, keep in mind that because of pollution you would not want to use the water maker in any of the crowded harbors in the Bahamas such as Lucaya, Nassau, Marsh Harbour, or Georgetown.

More important than a water maker is your water tank capacity. You should have at least 50 gallons capacity for each person on your vessel. The more, the better. Then you can fill up where available and not have to worry about running out. There is no reason to be more than 3 days away from fresh water at any time while in the Bahamas. Note, if your fresh water system uses filters, stock up prior to departing the US.

Carry a number of water jugs on your vessel. You can use them to store rainwater and to retrieve water from local wells and cisterns. A couple of 5-gallon water jugs should suffice.

Finally, develop a water catch system. When it rains you can catch the water yourself for free and have all you can hold. Most vessels carry some kind of canvas that can be rigged up so as to catch and funnel fresh rainwater into the vessels water tanks. On our trawler, we stored the hard dinghy right side up on the stern. When it rained, we would allow the rainwater to rinse out the dinghy and then put the stopper in the bottom. The dinghy then caught all the water it could hold. As soon as it was deep enough we placed a water hose in the dinghy and siphoned fresh water out and down into our water tanks. Simple but effective.

Some people frown on catching and drinking rainwater. Well surprise, surprise! The water you are paying $0.50 per gallon for probably fell on the roof of the marina and washed down into the gutter. From the gutter it went down a drainpipe into a large cistern. There it was stored until you pulled up to the dock and asked to fill up. That rainwater off the roof of the marina was then pumped into your boat's water tank. In all probability you will drink rainwater while in the Bahamas.

This leads to the last point about water in the Bahamas. We routinely add bleach to our water tanks each time we fill up. It doesn't take much to do the job. One teaspoon to fifty gallons is plenty. Of course this makes your water taste like chlorine. However, I have found that this is the least of your problems when it comes to the taste of drinking water. Drinking water from a boats water tank usually tastes awful even if you can't taste the chlorine. To combat this I installed a charcoal filter on the cold water line in the galley. That water tastes as fresh as mountain spring water all the time. It was cheap at $40, with replacement cartridges every six months for $10. Don't make the mistake of installing a filter with only a string sediment filter element. Make sure you get one that will use charcoal filter elements. It will be the best $40 you put into your boat.

It goes without saying that you should top off your water tanks before leaving for the Bahamas. If you insist on bottled drinking water, buy all you can carry before you leave. It won't get cheaper later.

Fuel

Fuel, both gasoline and diesel, is more expensive in the Bahamas. In November 2012 prices were about $1.50-$2.00/gallon higher than the east coast of Florida. Many marinas have a surcharge (as high as 5%) when a credit card is used. Of more concern is fuel quality. If you can, plan to fill up only in areas where a lot of sport fishing boats fill up and where a lot of fuel is routinely pumped. Make certain you use a "Bahamian-type" or "Baja" fuel filter.

Your dinghy motor usually has a separate fuel tank. Be sure it is filled with fresh fuel before you start for the Bahamas.

Diesel/Gas - $$$$$

Pump Out

Pump out facilities can be difficult to find and while a majority of the marinas do not offer this service, it is improving. Many of the big and newer marinas have slip pump out. In Marsh Harbour a pump out truck is sometimes available. Your vessel should be equipped with a treatment system such as Lectrasan or have the ability to empty the holding tank in open waters where it is authorized. Make certain that any modification you make to the sanitation system complies with US regulations.

GPS Plotters/Computer Navigation

Many Bahamas charts are based on the old, original British surveys and have not been updated. This may cause a discrepancy between your chart and your GPS location until your verify your chart. In addition, early electronic charts contained several errors. However, there are other suppliers who produce charts using their own survey data. Explorer Charts and NV-Charts produce chart books while Wavey Line Publishing produces individual charts. Make certain you have the most recent editions and carry the appropriate paper charts as a back- up. And make certain your chart plotter is set to the proper Datum for the charts/cartridges you are using.

Charts and Cruising Guides

Appendix A lists the charts and cruising guides you need to go to the Bahamas. It is important to note that you do not need all of these charts and cruising guides if you are going to limit your trip to one area. In chapter 2 I discuss two possible destinations for your trip. If you feel you will probably only go to one of these areas you can save money by not buying the charts and cruising guides for the other area. I have identified which charts and guides you need for each area in the Bahamas. You should purchase those that you feel you will need prior to your departure. While it is possible to find them in the Bahamas, I have found that it can be difficult and certainly more expensive.

If you feel you may cruise extensively in the Bahamas and/or do so for a few years to come, it probably is a good idea to just buy them all now. This not only insures that you have all of them when you need them, it allows you to study them now. As you study them you may decide to go to an area that originally was not in your plans, just based on what you read. Also, you may only plan on going to the Abacos, however, once there you may make friends with another boat and decide to travel with them on to Eleuthera and/or the Exumas.

Until the GPS came along, charts for the Bahamas were relatively old and in many cases showed locations more than a mile from their actual position. With todays navigation software and accurate paper charts, travel among the islands is not difficult. In addition, some cruising guides like the Waterway Guide Bahamas edition and Steve Dodge's Abaco guide provide very good GPS waypoints of crucial locations. That said, minor errors do creep in when producing these documents and you should always travel in daylight hours under good visibility conditions whenever you first travel in any area in the Bahamas!

I was talking to a fellow cruiser one day and he told me his GPS was wacky. I asked him why and he told me when he plotted his position according to his GPS he was in the middle of the island. I had to explain to him that the GPS was correct. The older chart he was using was wrong. You cannot calculate waypoints from the older charts and use them in your GPS for close navigation in the Bahamas. You must use the validated information you will find in the cruising guides and newer charts I have recommended for accurate navigation points.

Cigarettes

Cigarettes and cigars are very expensive in the Bahamas. If you smoke you will want to carry as many as you may think you will use while there. If you are a cigar smoker and want to try a Cuban cigar, you will get the opportunity in the Bahamas. Many places sell Cuban cigars as there are no restrictions.

Drinks

Beer and Soda is very expensive in the Bahamas. Beer runs $40 and up per case and soda runs up to $6 per 6 pack. If you drink either you may want to carry as much as you can up to and including enough to last your trip to the Bahamas. Diet soda provides a unique problem. Diet soda, unlike regular soda, has a shelf life of only about twelve months. If stocking up for many months, be sure the diet soda you buy is fresh. If you don't the artificial sweetener may

Beer is $40/case.

"turn" and you will have some of the most horrible tasting colored carbonated water you can imagine.

Wine and hard liquor is also more expensive. The exceptions are locally made rum and hard liquor not made in the U.S. So provison prior to your departure.

Food

Almost all food in the Bahamas costs more than in the states. There are a few locally grown items available in various locations. They include chickens, eggs, pork, and some garden vegetables like tomatoes and peppers. However, even these foods cost a little more than in the states. Most foods are available in the local grocery. However, since many of these stores are very small, your selection may be limited. Also, it is not uncommon for stores to run out of goods on Sunday and Monday prior to the new deliveries. In the larger cities like Nassau, Marsh Harbour and Georgetown you can find just about any food item you want in the larger stores. It's just a matter of how much you are willing to pay.

Canned goods are straightforward. Buy as much as you think you may use and carry it low in the boat. In addition to the normal canned vegetables and soups, look for things like canned hams, chicken and beef that do not have to be refrigerated. You will find some canned meats in the supermarkets in Florida, however for a reliable source you may want to order directly from a company that specializes in canned meats. One good source for canned beef, pork, chicken and turkey is Werling and Sons, Inc., 100 South Plum Street, Burkettsville, OH 45310. Telephone 1-888-375-1998, or www.werlingandsons.com. Another source for canned meats is Brinkman Turkey Farms, Inc., 16314 US Route 68, Findlay, OH 45840, 1-419-365-5127, or www.brinkmanfarms.com. They are a bit more expensive but some boaters feel their meat is a little better quality and they do offer the option of salt free meats.

Both companies will mix or match different meats in case lots of 12 cans each for the same price as all one-type meat. Food in boxes is pretty safe. We routinely stock up on cereal, pancake mix, instant potatoes, etc with no problem. We store these in dry compartments about midway up on our vessel.

Flour seems to develop bugs after a period and we have taken to "nuking" our flour when we buy it. We put a 5-pound bag of flour in the microwave for 5 minutes and then stick it in a large zip lock bag. This seems to defeat the critters in all commercial flour. Sugar doesn't need to be nuked, but is also inserted in a large zip lock bag to keep it dry and fresh.

Fresh meat is the biggest problem. Unless you buy canned beef, chicken, pork, or turkey, you are limited to the storage capacity of your freezer. We buy only the best cut of meat and pack it in individual 8 oz packages (4 oz for each of us). These are then stuck in our freezer. We find we can get 40 packages like this in our freezer. While there we eat some meals containing canned meat (tuna, salmon, and ham), and we eat out on occasion. This extends our meats for meals to about 80 or almost 3 months. Add to this fresh fish that we catch and/or buy from a local fisherman and we easily carry enough meat for 90 days or three months.

While there we augment our food stores with purchases from local farmers (tomatoes, green peppers, etc.), local fisherman (grouper, conch, etc), local bakery (bread, cakes, etc.) and finally from the supermarket when we have too.

We thought milk would be a real problem, but were pleasantly surprised to find irradiated milk in boxes in supermarkets in Florida. These one-quart size milk containers come in whole,

1% and skim and have an expiration date of about six months. We carry this milk un-refrigerated until just before we open it and of course we keep it refrigerated while using it.

Appendix 2 is a sample list of what we stock for 3 months. It will vary dramatically for different boaters. Be sure to stock up with as much food as you can carry before leaving for the Bahamas. This will save you a lot in your food costs.

Eating out is always an option. However, eating out in the Bahamas can be very expensive. A lot depends on the location you choose, just as in the states. A chicken dinner can cost $20 to $25. A hamburger is usually $8 to $10. Steak and lobster dinners are $35. Anything you eat out is more expensive. Remember the restaurant you are eating in must pay the higher price for all of its food and of course passes this cost on to you.

Ships Stores and Customs

Anything you carry on your vessel is considered "ships stores". You are not required to pay any customs duty on any ships stores. However, ships stores are intended to be consumed on your vessel. You are not allowed to sell, trade or barter your ships stores with anyone unless you first pay duty on these items.

It is true that cruisers often "share" their wealth with fellow cruisers and on occasion have a potluck dinner or provide that important can of kidney beans for someone else's chili. These innocent transgressions tend to be overlooked. However, do not think you can carry a large quantify of one item over there and sell it at a profit. If you get caught the penalty is severe, up to and including the seizure of your vessel!

Telephone

A lot of information on telephone use, including cell phones, in the Bahamas is given in Chapter 5. A satellite phone is another option and the website for the Satellite Phone Store gives information about renting a satellite phone from them. These folks have both Iridium and Inmarset phones available. It should be noted that several cruisers have reported only marginal success using satellite phones.

Medical Services

As one might expect where the population is concentrated in just a few locations and the remainder spread over many islands and miles, medical services will vary greatly. In the two largest centers, Nassau and Freeport/Lucaya, you will find modern hospitals, up-to-date dental clinics and access to well educated health care professionals. In Nassau there are two main hospitals; the government owned Princell Margaret Hospital, and the ever expanding privately owned Doctors Hospital. In Freeport there is the Rand Memorial Hospital In Marsh Harbour there is a government clinic and several local doctors and there are plans to open a hospital. The only hyperbaric chamber is at Lyford Cay Hospital, together with the Bahamas Heart Institute. Throughout the smaller, more remote areas you will find clinics staffed by a nurse and/or physician who are able to handle most things except very serious injuries or illness. In very small villages the clinics will be staffed by a part-time nurse.

Dental care is also available but it is most likely to be found in the more densely populated areas.

Medical and dental care is very expensive and in most instances U.S. medical insurance policies are not accepted. Payment in cash is expected. Check with your insurance carrier regarding any coverage you may have prior to departing.

Prescription drug refills generally are not an issue and most of the time refills will not count toward the number you have remaining on a specific prescription. Pharmacists will recommend products for treatment and in many instances will offer medication "over the counter" that would require a prescription in the U.S. As with medical and dental care, expect to pay cash.

Chapter 4
The Crossing

It all comes down to this. "The Crossing." How you handle the crossing will determine whether this is a good trip or a bad one. It will probably decide whether your first mate ever allows you to go to the Bahamas again. Careful planning and care is required in selecting where you cross from and what day you choose to cross. Your boat is provisioned. You have more than a month available. You are ready to go.

It is important to note that the **information contained herein is not to be used for navigation**. Prudent boaters will use the current charts, appropriate navigation aids, recent notice to mariners, and electronic navigation equipment while operating their vessel. The most recent changes due to shoaling, sunken vessels, etc. cannot be and <u>will not</u> be found in this publication.

The first step is to decide where you will cross from and where you will cross to. In other words, the route to the Bahamas. A lot of decisions will be made for you by the type of boat you have and where you have chosen to go. For purposes of this book, I will assume you are located on the east coast of Florida and want to cross to either the northern or southern Bahamas. With that in mind, you can get to just about anywhere in the Bahamas with ease.

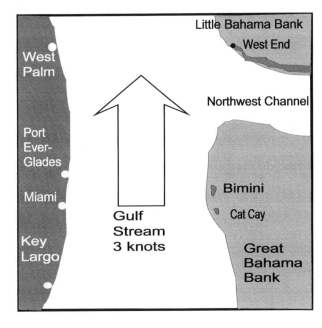

The drawing at the right depicts the problem. If you have decided to visit the northern Bahamas you can depart from any point in Florida from West Palm Beach south to Key Largo. Obviously the further south you go, the longer the journey. On the other side of that same coin is the fact that the Gulf Stream plays an important part in your journey; particularly for a slower vessel. If you cross from West Palm Beach directly to West End on the Grand Bahama Island your course over ground (COG) must be nearly due east. The Gulf Stream is going to set your boat to the north by a considerable amount. Thus the course you must steer will be southeast.

If you depart from a point as far south as Key Largo, then the Gulf Stream acts more to increase your boat speed than it does to offset it to the north. In other words it actually pushes you towards West End faster and your speed over ground (SOG) actually increases.

To further complicate matters, the Gulf Stream is not as wide as the space between the two landmasses, Florida and the Bahama Banks, instead averaging only 25 miles. Thus, in the middle, the Gulf Stream is flowing 3 knots, but near the edge it is less than 1 knot. Worse still, outside the Gulf Stream right next to shore, you may actually see a slight southern current.

Do not underestimate the effect of the Gulf Stream. Not only does it offset your course to the north, but it also creates a real hazard when it comes to wind and waves. Because of its northward movement any wind with a north component tends to oppose the flow of the Gulf Stream. This causes the water in the Gulf Stream to stand up in very large short waves. While a 15-knot wind may normally cause 5-foot waves in the open ocean, that same 15-knot wind from the north may cause 10-foot waves in the Gulf Stream. For this reason, all crossings to the Bahamas should be made in winds that do not have a northern component; i.e. NW through N to NE. Instead you should select a day when the winds are light SE through S to W. For trawlers a flat calm day is preferred. For sailboats that desire to sail, winds from the SW to W are ideal.

Preparing to Cross

Because of the Gulf Stream your starting point should be some point due west or southwest of your ending point. Thus if you decide to cross to West End on the Grand Bahama Island (or Memory Rock) you would start at West Palm Beach, Port Everglades or even Miami (though not normally that far south). If you decide to cross to Bimini on the Great Bahama Bank (or Cat Cay) you would start at Miami or near Key Largo. You would not normally ever start very much north of the point you wanted to end up at. If you did, you would have a much longer journey, time wise, due to the Gulf Stream.

The Explorer Chartbook Near Bahamas and the Waterway Guide Bahamas 2013 Edition give detailed routes to the Bahamas with waypoints, distances, and compass headings. Appendix B also gives course information. But you just can't follow those headings and in the following paragraphs I am going to explain the navigation problem you encounter and how best to solve it.

First pick your starting point. If going to the northern Bahamas the preferred starting point is Lake Worth at West Palm Beach. You can stay in a marina there or anchor in Lake Worth while waiting for a weather window. Optionally you could go south to Fort Lauderdale or Hollywood and anchor or stay in a marina there. You would use the Port Everglades inlet as your departure point. It is further, 69.1 nautical miles versus 54.1 nautical miles from the Lake Worth Inlet to West End. However, because of the Gulf Stream assist, the time to make the passage is almost identical for slower boats.

Some cruisers do start even further south and even north of Lake Worth. The necessary navigational information is given in both the chart kit I referenced and the appropriate cruising guide. However, I don't recommend it for the cruiser on the first crossing.

If your destination is the southern Bahamas you should be looking at crossing to Bimini or Cat Cay on the Great Bahama Bank. Your starting point of choice should be in Miami area where there is ample anchorage in Hurricane or No Name Harbor or you can stay in one of the marinas in Miami or Miami Beach. Your departure from Government Cut would necessitate a journey of 42 nautical miles to either Bimini or Cat Cay. In addition you could stay further south in the Florida Keys and get more of an assist from the Gulf Stream in your crossing. A departure from an inlet near Key Largo will entail a journey of 53 nautical miles to Bimini and about 51 nautical miles to Cat Cay.

Make your decision and move your vessel to your chosen starting point. Keep in mind you may be there for any time from one day to two or three weeks waiting for a good weather window.

Plotting Your Crossing

As previously mentioned, Appendix B lists several recommended crossing routes with heading and distance information and the estimated enroute times at various speeds.

No matter where you choose to start from the problem is the same. How do you account for the Gulf Stream during your crossing? There are three approaches to plotting the crossing. First, and probably the least preferred method is to plot a course directly to your destination and forget about the Gulf Stream. Let's assume you left from Lake Worth and headed for West End on the Grand Bahama Island. It is 54.1 nautical miles on a heading of 98 degrees. If you start across maintaining a heading of 98M degrees and your vessel averages 6 knots, it will take you 9 hours to make the crossing. Unfortunately your first sight of land will place you about 16 nautical miles north of West End or right about White Sand Ridge on the Little Bahama Bank. You would then have to turn almost due south for 16 miles and 2 ¾ hours before you would arrive at West End. Total time of the trip would be about 11 ¾ hours. Ignoring the Gulf Stream offset is not the way to go.

The second method of plotting your course, and the most popular method used today, is letting your GPS do all the work for you. You enter the waypoint for West End in your GPS. It shows a course over ground (COG) of 98 degrees and a distance to West End of 54.1 nautical miles. When you depart the Lake Worth Inlet, your GPS tells you to keep heading 98 degrees. Shortly thereafter your GPS may indicate that your course made good (CMG) is perhaps 105 degrees. Even though you are steering 98 degrees you may be pushed slightly south. This is due to the slight eddy current from the Gulf Stream that actually flows south very close to shore in Florida. Soon however, your vessel begins to feel the northern effects of the Gulf Stream and your CMG will decrease towards 90 degrees. You will have to steer further and further south to achieve a CMG of 98 degrees, which is what you want to reach West End. As you are pushed faster and faster towards the north, traveling at 6 knots you will have to steer 110, 120 and even 125 degrees to make up for the offset the Gulf Stream.

When you reach the center of the Gulf Stream the 3-knot northern current forces you three knots north for every 6 knots you go east. To offset this, you have to steer 126 degrees to achieve a CMG of 98 degrees. You continue to steer for the West End waypoint and maintain whatever heading is necessary to achieve a CMG of 98 degrees. The closer you get to the Little Bahama Bank, the weaker the Gulf Stream becomes and you begin to steer closer to 98 degrees to achieve 98 degrees. When the Gulf Stream is down to 2 knots you steer 117 degrees for a CMG of 98 and at one knot in the Gulf Stream you steer 108 degrees for a CMG of 98 degrees.

The effect of all of this is that it actually takes you longer to make the crossing than the 9 hours you calculated. When the Gulf Stream was at its strongest, 3 knots, your speed over ground (SOG) was no longer the 6 knots your knotmeter showed. It would only be 5.3 knots. This loss of SOG comes from the fact that you are "crabbing" or heading into the current to offset the error caused by the sideways current. We all are familiar with this effect when we cross a river, like the Savannah. Crossing the Savannah River we have to aim for a point to the left or right of the channel entrance on the other side to allow for the perpendicular flow of the river. You have to do the same thing to achieve the COG calculated by your GPS for crossing the Gulf Stream.

Have I confused you with all the facts? If I have, keep it simple. Put a waypoint in your GPS and head for it. Continue to steer more to the south as necessary to make the course you want while crossing so that you will end up at the waypoint you want. What I had hoped to accomplish was to explain to you why your "GPS seems wacky" when crossing and it actually isn't. Also to explain why the 54-mile trip will take closer to 10 hours than the 9 hours you calculated at 6 knots.

The third method of crossing can actually shave some time off your crossing once you understand the problem as I have explained it above. When you are steering 126 degrees to make 98 degrees your SOG drops almost a knot at 6 knots to only 5.3 knots. At 117 degrees you are actually making 5.5 knots, and at 108 degrees you're SOG is 5.8 knots. Simply put, if you never had to steer as much as 28 degrees south, you could increase your speed by 0.7 knots. The fact is, that you cannot ignore the Gulf Stream and make landfall at your chosen destination. However, if you don't attempt to maintain a straight-line course to the Bahamas you can increase your average SOG. Here is how it works.

Instead of leaving Lake Worth and trying to maintain a course over ground (COG) of 98 degrees by adjusting our heading further and further south as the GPS tells us we are drifting north, we ignore the GPS. (Blasphemy you say!) We actually figure out the course we would have to sail to achieve our destination accounting only for an offset by the Gulf Stream. We know that the Gulf Steam heads north at speeds from –0.5 to 3 knots. We also know that as we cross the Gulf Stream it is weakest at the edges and strongest in the middle. If you were to plot

the cross section of the current at ½ mile intervals it would go from –0.5 to 0, to 0.5 and up to 3.0 in the middle (assuming a normal day). Finally it would decrease again from 3.0 in the middle to 0 and actually a small negative value as you approached landfall in the Bahamas.

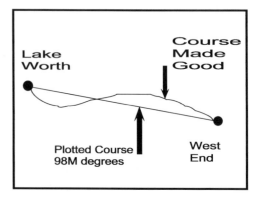

To further complicate matters the Gulf Stream actually moves slightly east to west and expands and contracts throughout the year depending on the volume of water moving north. So there are no absolute numbers available. However, you can estimate the numbers well enough to solve this problem. For purposes of our calculations assume that the average speed of the Gulf Stream is 1.8 knots from Lake Worth to West End with the top speed of 3.0 knots. If we plan our 54.1 nautical mile crossing based on average speed of the Gulf Stream of 1.8 knots, and travel at 6 knots, we would see an offset of nearly 16.3 nautical miles. To offset 16.3 miles we would have to take a heading of 115 degrees instead of 98 degrees. The result of our journey is shown in the plot above.

When you first leave Lake Worth your track or course made good (CMG) will actually go south of the projected course over ground (COG). But as the Gulf Stream kicks in, the vessel will drift further north since the course you are steering is not offset enough to account for the full effect of the Gulf Stream. Eventually as you head east you begin to make ground over the effect of the Gulf Stream and end up at your projected waypoint. Since you never had to take a heading of 26 degrees below the COG your speed over ground (SOG) never dropped to 5.3 knots. Instead at all times you averaged a higher SOG using this method as opposed to the one where you blindly follow the GPS instructions. This can shave between one half hour and an hour off your crossing time.

The table at the right shows the number of degrees to add to the COG heading from two starting points in Florida to both West End and Bimini. If you desire to land at a different point in the Bahamas you can use the same number from the chart to calculate the correct heading for that point. For locations in the same approximate vicinity use the number shown and add it to the magnetic heading as calculated by your GPS.

	Heading Magnetic	Speed in knots						
		5	6	7	8	9	10	11
Lake Worth to West End	98°	20	17	15	13	12	11	10
Miami to Bimini	110°	23	19	17	15	14	12	11

Here is an example of how to use the chart on the previous page. You are going from Lake Worth to West End. Your vessel travels at an average speed of 5.5 knots. The magnetic heading from Lake Worth is 98 degrees. At 5.5 knots, add between 20 (5 knots) and 17 (6 knots) degrees, or about 18.5 degrees. You would try to maintain a heading of 116.5 degrees in route to West End.

Suppose you choose to go to Cat Cay from Miami instead of Bimini. Your average boat speed is 6.5 knots. The heading from Miami to Cat Cay is 110 degrees. At 6.5 knots from the above chart we add half way between 6 and 7 knots, or 18 degrees. The correct heading from Miami to Cat Cay is 110 plus 18, or 128 degrees at 6.5 knots.

In either event, as you approach landfall and your waypoint you can be sure you will not be exactly where you want to be. Differences in Gulf Stream currents and width, winds, your vessel speed, etc. assure you of this. As you get within 2-3 miles of your waypoint, switch from the calculated heading to the heading given at that time on your GPS or Loran. This will insure the final correction as you approach landfall and put you right on the mark.

Final Plotting Decision

Human nature tends to keep us from doing things that look wrong. Thus, if you choose the last method to get to the Bahamas, you will save some time in the crossing. You may however, have a difficult time convincing your crew. Further, it is normal for anxiety to creep up, and maintaining a heading that your GPS keeps telling you is wrong can really frustrate some people. If you can't use the last method outlined above to maintain your course to the Bahamas, then by all means, use the 2nd method outlined above. It will take you a little longer to get there, but is easier to sell to the crew and generally makes everyone feel better about where they are steering.

A Buddy Boat

You have everything ready. All the provisions are aboard. You have decided your course and heading. The charts are laid out and ready. You put out a call on VHF channel 16, "Anyone interested in traveling to the Bahamas switch and answer channel 72". You stand by. With any luck several boats will come up on the radio. These may be in addition to any number of vessels you have been talking to first hand in your anchorage area or marina. Now is the time to arrange to travel with one or more other boats to the Bahamas. The first concern is how fast the boat travels. You want to find buddy boats that travel at nearly the same speed as you. We have on occasion slowed down or increased our speed to stay with one or more boats.

The next question is where do they want to make landfall in the Bahamas. It does no good to try to buddy boat with someone that wants to head to Freeport from Lake Worth if you are going to West End. Then comes the matter of their readiness. You want to be able to go the first moment you get a good weather window. You don't want to commit to going with some boat that has yet to provision or is waiting for additional crewmembers. They have to be ready to go now, the same as you.

Finally, you must discuss the matter of a weather window. You don't want to wait with a boat that is willing to go with 15-knot winds from the north if you want a really easy ride. Make sure the boats you line up as buddy boats have the same philosophy as you with regard to the weather window.

Meet with any and all that seem likely candidates. Discuss your final destinations and why you are going the way you are. Make sure you are compatible with anyone you agree to buddy boat with. Discuss the rules pertaining to assisting one another. If one boat breaks down, will another one tow it? If one boat has to turn back, do all boats have to turn back? In the end you should find one or two boats willing to travel with you as a buddy boat that will respond to your needs and make you feel more comfortable on this exciting adventure. The last time I crossed the Gulf Stream I did so in the company of six other trawlers all headed from West End to Lake Worth. It was a great trip. We told jokes on the VHF on low power and got to know each other real well. More importantly we all knew that if one of us broke down there were six others there willing to jump in and help.

The inclination is to go it alone and not worry about a buddy boat. We have done it both ways. I can tell you that having a friend on the endless horizon sure goes a long way to allowing the crew to relax during this open ocean crossing.

The Weather Window

What is a good "Weather Window"? Simply put, it is weather with winds and seas that satisfy your level of comfort and safety while making an open ocean crossing of the Gulf Stream. A good weather window for one boat may not be a good weather window for another boat. Case in point. I was talking to a sailboat captain in Lake Worth waiting to cross. When we got to the "weather window", he was very emphatic. He wanted 15-20 knots out of the SW or W so he could sail. He was concerned that with his slow sailboat, it would take forever to get to West End if he had to go by motor alone. He and I were not compatible when it comes to weather windows.

I have a trawler. "No wind" is more to my liking. Unfortunately that is rare and it has only happened to me twice in seven years. Rather, I have set limits for myself. No winds from the north. I mean zero. Light winds from the SE through S to W of 10 knots or less. Reported seas of 2 feet or less. Can you get these ideal conditions? Absolutely! Is it easy? No.

To get a good weather window you first need a source for weather information. Satellite TV and the Weather Channel is an excellent start. In lieu of that, local TV channels often give good weather information, but you may have to watch several newscasts to get a good picture of the weather showing isobars. Seeing a weather map with isobars is the key. Of course if you have weather fax you are in great shape. Listening to the weather channel on the VHF radio is also a

Picture of a great crossing. Our buddy boat can be seen making way in almost mirror like conditions after a two day calm.

help. However, I only use the VHF weather channel to confirm what I have already figured out from other sources. I never depend on the VHF weather channel for actual weather forecasts. I just find the VHF weather channel wrong too often.

Another option is the Internet. If you have access there are a number of good web sites that provide information on weather. I like the site that gives the readings at the ocean buoys. It is the National Data Buoy Center, http://ndbc.noaa.gov. With this site I can look at the actual wind conditions for the last 24 hours both at Lake Worth and West End. Here is a hint. The weather today at Lake Worth is pretty much what the weather will be in 6 hours at West End. I also like to go to the NOAA marine weather site and see the printed marine weather forecast at http://www.weather.gov/om/marine/home.htm. Weather Underground,www.wunderground.com is another good site. There is also a site in the Bahamas that you might want to try: www.bahamasweather.org.bs. If you are departing from Lake Worth, you might find a sailboat waiting to cross that has a forecast from a private service such as Chris Parker (chris@mwxc.com). Finally, you might have or want to subscribe to one of the satellite weather services such as WxWorx or Sirius Marine Weather Service.

Let's run through Weather Forecasting 101. Weather is controlled by Highs and Lows. Wind circulates the Highs in a clockwise direction and the Lows in a counter clockwise direction. The area where the winds switch direction is called a front. Fronts generally travel east but also slide north or south of that track. The tighter (closer) the isobars around a High or Low (difference of pressure), the greater the wind speed. If a low is imbedded on the front, there are usually storms accompanying the front passage. Storms normally occur just as a front passes. Storms rarely occur in an area controlled by a High.

In the winter months the weather in Florida and the Bahamas follows a very predictable pattern. The cycle starts with the passage of a front. If a Low is imbedded in the front, you may have rain and storms. However, often a cold front passes without rain. Just as soon as the front passes your location (usually moving east) the winds will shift to the NW at 20-25 knots and the temperatures will drop. Over the next few days the winds "clock around" first to the N then NE and E. The winds generally begin to diminish then to 10-15 knots and continue "clocking" to the SE, S, and then SW. When the winds reach the SW another cold front is sure to be on the horizon. Sometimes there will be a little rain ahead of the front called pre-frontal activity. Normally the bad weather comes with the passage of the front and the cycle begins again.

On occasion a front stalls and you can be anywhere in the cycle when this happens. If it stalls to the north of you, you may have sustained E or SE winds for several days. Also a High can slow down or stall right over you. In that case you may have beautiful warm weather for several days with almost no wind. However, it is not normal for the weather pattern to stall in your area and for the most part the cycle described above will repeat itself every 3-4 days.

The most ideal scenario for us, when waiting for a good weather window, has a High pass directly over us. The center of the High is very wide, at least several hundred miles. I have seen High pressure areas where the first (inner most) isobar extends from the west coast of Florida to the Abacos. As this High approaches the winds will drop to light from the NE less than 5 knots. Then the forecast will be light and variable less than 5 knots. Finally the winds will be forecast from the SW light, less than 5 knots. With a slow moving High such as this you have about as ideal weather pattern as you can get. Light winds, no chance of storms, and plenty of time.

It isn't enough that the forecast be for good weather. The weather window also has to last long enough for the ocean to settle down and you to get across. If the winds have been blowing pretty strong for several days, the ocean will have some substantial waves and they do not disappear the minute the winds abate. Allow at least 24 hours after strong winds before going out on the ocean. This gives the ocean time to lie down.

Make sure it is not a fast moving weather system. You want at least 2 days before the winds pick back up as the front passes. When you see what appears to be a good window approaching study all your weather sources closely. Discuss it with fellow cruisers waiting to cross. If it is Sunday and it appears the winds will drop on Monday, then perhaps you can move on Tuesday. If the winds drop on Monday as forecast, check out the buoy reports on the VHF weather channel. What winds and wave heights are being reported? By Monday night you are ready to make your final decision. If the winds have remained light all day (Monday) as forecast, the most recent buoy reports should be for small wave heights in the Gulf Stream (Less than 5 feet). If the winds remain light again Monday night, the waves will drop even further by departure time on Tuesday.

Departure should be very early in the morning. This ensures you will arrive at West End or Bimini in daylight hours. You should never try to make landfall in the Bahamas during nighttime hours. Channel markers are almost nonexistent. Navigation lights spotty to none at all. Do not try to arrive in the Bahamas at night! We often leave at 4 or 5 AM so that we will arrive 9 hours later in West End or Bimini at 1 or 2 PM. At that time of day the sun is past the zenith and at our back, ensuring good visibility. You may need the visibility to read the waters for depth.

Time to Move

The weather looks good. It has been relatively calm all day. The ocean is lying down. The forecast is for light winds 10 knots or less from the SW tomorrow switching to 5 knots from the west in the afternoon. The next front is not due until two days from now. All of your buddy boats have agreed. This is a go. Now is a good time to move from your more protected anchorage to a point closer to the inlet. You will be leaving in the early morning hours before daylight so as to arrive around 1 PM. From the Lake Worth anchorage most vessels move down to an anchorage just south of the inlet. Less protected, it is fine for that one night with light winds. It gives you easy access to the inlet in the dark morning hours.

In the Miami area you might choose to move from No Name Harbor to a marina in South Miami Beach. Be sure to check dockage rates. Here you can fill your water tanks, get some last minute provisions, and have an easy shot out Government Cut in the dark morning hours.

All of the buddy boats agree on a time to begin movement with a projected time to clear the inlet. A typical plan might call for raising the anchor at 4 AM and clear the inlet by 5 AM.

To insure that everyone is on the same sheet of music, we usually agree to monitor some specific VHF radio channel that night, other than 16. The first boat to get up at the appointed time puts out a call to insure everyone is getting ready. Once you have established communications with all other vessels confirm the time to begin movement. Things may be going well and you might want to leave 30 minutes earlier. On the other side of the coin, one of the vessels may be having trouble stowing their dinghy and decide they need an additional 30 minutes.

In any event this VHF radio channel becomes the group's working channel for the crossing. Most vessels can monitor two channels at once. Thus you set your VHF radio to monitor channel 16 and the agreed upon channel, say 72. At the agreed upon time you all move out headed for the inlet.

The Crossing

It is normal to be apprehensive about crossing the Gulf Stream. Even though we cruised about 5,000 miles each year, our crossing the Gulf Stream twice each year was the most stressful time we had. Both going over and coming back, cause equal concern. We were not so much frightened that we would lose our vessel. Rather it was the knowledge that we could be in for an uneventful and pleasant day or we might experience 9-10 hours of pure misery. As we learned to master the weather window, our crossings became easier and more pleasant. Unfortunately like so many of you will, we figured on our first crossing, "How bad can 20 knot winds on the nose be?" What a mistake. Our vessel handled the seas with ease, but the crew did not!

As you head out the inlet, the seas should be very calm. It is early morning and the winds in the dark hours are usually 5 knots less than what will come in the daytime. We usually experience almost dead calm conditions when starting out. If not, check that weather forecast again. Something may have changed. There will always be a swell coming in with a long time period, but nothing to cause you a problem. When you first get on the ocean it is a good time to check in with all your buddy boats. Check for targets on your radar or AIS. (AIS stands for Automatic Identification System and consists of transmitters/receivers that broadcast and display vessel tracking and indentification information). Verify that each boat has the same waypoint plotted into their GPS. The GPS solution should be nearly identical for each vessel. As an example, if leaving Government Cut for Cat Cay, they should indicate the waypoint at about 110M and 43.7 nautical miles. Ask everyone to switch his or her VHF radios to low power. As the day drags on, a lot of chitchat will occur on your selected working channel and there is no point interfering with other boaters.

The first couple of miles will decide if you want to continue that day. If the ocean is still rough because it has not had time to lie down or some distant wind is stirring it up you may want to return to your safe harbor immediately. The trip will not get easier! As you approach the Gulf Stream you will encounter the worst the ocean has to offer that day. If you have 2-foot waves close to shore, plan on 4-foot waves in the center of the Gulf Stream. If the ocean is relatively flat and the winds light, you should continue on.

When we first leave the inlet I make a point of noting the time and position from my GPS on my chart. Thereafter I record the time and position every hour. If you are following the second navigation solution, you will end up plotting a nearly perfect straight line from your starting point to your waypoint. Of course if you have been bold and selected the 3rd navigation method outlined above, your plot will more closely represent a large lazy S on its side.

During the crossing, check in regularly with all buddy boats. You should not experience any unusual weather if you have done your weather window homework correctly. However, one of the boats may experience engine difficulties. Then it is time to act according to your buddy boat plan. Tow the problem boat, sit in the water and wait for help, slow down and proceed at the speed the disabled boat can make, etc. Once you have reached the halfway point your options about going back disappear and now you should only consider continuing on or seeking help from the Bahamas end.

If you have the instrumentation to measure water temperature, you will note a significant rise in water temperature when you enter the Gulf Stream. While it may be as cold as 70 near Florida shores it will rise to 75 to 80 degrees in the middle of the stream. At about the same time you will also lose the use of your depth finder. When the water depths drop to thousands of feet all depth finders fail.

If you have an emergency and a "buddy boat" cannot assist, help will most likely come from the U.S. Coast Guard or the Bahamas Air Sea Rescue Association (BASRA). BASRA should not be compared to the Coast Guard in its ability to provide rescue services. It is a non- profit all volunteer organization dedicated to assisting distressed seamen and airmen in The Bahamas. But its services are limited. BASRA monitors VHF Channel 16 and SSB 2182 from 9 am to 5 pm daily. Outside of those hours you contact the U. S. Coast Guard on SSB 2182 and Nassau Harbor Control or The Royal Bahamas Defense Force on VHF Channel 16. For more information on BASRA visit their website, www.basra.org.

Land Fall

As you proceed east from Florida you will be able to make out lights and buildings for about 10 miles. Then there will be nothing on the horizon except the running lights of fellow cruisers or other vessels passing in the night. Remember that these waters are plied by large ocean going ships and they will NOT make an effort to avoid you. Be sure to keep out of their way.

The water will become a dark blue color unlike anything you have ever seen in US waters. As daylight comes on you may see flying fish leaping out of the water in all directions off your bow. In addition you may encounter some dolphins. If you are into fishing, now is a good time as I have outlined in Chapter 3.

About 10 miles from your projected waypoint in the Bahamas you should begin to see funny dots and shapes on the horizon. Eventually these dots will fill in and the outline of trees and islands will appear. When you get down to less than 3 miles confirm your waypoint settings again and insure you are all headed for the same point. This is also a good time to raise your quarantine flag and alert your fellow buddy boats to do the same.

While crossing, your depth finder went into overload and may have blinked error or some ridiculous number. However as you get closer to land, the bottom will start to come up from thousands of feet to hundreds and your depth finder will again begin to function. That is when you know for sure you have made it. You are about to experience something that is truly beautiful and scary at the same time. The water is so clear as you approach landfall you can easily see down 10-20 feet, and 60-70 feet if the sea is glassy. On a calm day in less than 10 feet it is difficult to judge the water depth because the water is so clear.

While in the Bahamas you will have to learn to "read" the water depth by its color. Suffice it to say that this takes some time before you build up your confidence and come to recognize deeper water and shallow water or reefs. In the meantime, on that first landfall when entering an obviously shallow channel you can't help but be apprehensive about how much water is available. The most important advice is to rely on your navigation tools, your charts and most importantly, the three recommended cruising guides. In these cruising guides you will find detailed instructions on how to enter each harbor in the area covered. These cruising guides are indispensable for safe navigation in the Bahamas.

Clearing Customs

Once in the safety of the harbor secure your vessel while you clear customs. In all cases you can tie up to a marina with your yellow quarantine flag displayed and ask the dockmaster about clearing customs. The dockmaster will make arrangements for you to either go to the customs office or have the customs personnel come to your vessel.

It is a good idea to have all the necessary information at the ready. Have the following:

- Ships documentation, either Coast Guard document or state registration (have an **extra copy** to give the customs official)
- Passports, photo drivers license, or birth certificate for each crew member
- If you have weapons, the make, model and serial number of each weapon
- If you have any ammunition, the caliper and exact number of rounds
- For your dinghy, the registration
- For your dinghy motor, the make, HP, and serial number
- For a computer, the make, model and serial number
- For motor scooters or motor cycles, the registration
- For bicycles, the make, model and serial number

While the above list is pretty complete, you also may be asked about some other specific thing they are checking on. As certain items become of real value in the Bahamas the customs personnel like to note them on your cruising permit. They might at some future point check on satellite TV, GPS or anything else.

The forms are lengthy, but easy to fill out and once done for a fee, you and your crew are cleared to be in the Bahamas.

The process for obtaining a cruising permit is worth repeating.

The fee for vessels with 4 person or less 35' and under is $150. For vessels over 35' it is $300. Dinghies over 18' are charged $150. This fee covers the captain and up to three additional crewmembers. Above that the fee is $15 per head. Be sure and get a receipt for any fee you pay. This fee also covers the $15 fee people are charged that return to the states via airplane. This will save you $15 if you have to fly back. Further, at this time the fee paid covers a second entry to the Bahamas in any 90-day period. Thus, if something comes up and you take your boat back to the US, but later want to come back to the Bahamas within 90 days, you will not have to pay a second cruising permit fee. Note: These fees were in effect November 2011. Check www.bahamas.com/bahamas/regulations-0 for updates.

You get two permits to enter the Bahamas. One is a cruising permit, normally good for 12 months. The other is your immigration permit. If your port of entry has only one official serving as both a Customs and Immigration officer, you will probably get an immigration permit valid for 90 days. If there are separate officials then you will probably receive a 12 month immigration permit.

The fee also includes a fishing license for you and all your crewmembers for the three months. An additional three months fishing license can be had for $150. Finally, there are no restrictions on any items you have brought into the Bahamas as part of ships stores and you will rarely be asked any questions about them. You may be asked if you "brought anything into the country for anyone else?" Of course the answer should be no. Customs and immigration clearance should not take more than an hour from start to finish.

When you return to your vessel, lower the quarantine flag and raise the Bahamas courtesy flag. Welcome to the Bahamas, Mon! All ashore, that is going ashore.

Chapter 5
While There

You made it to the Bahamas! And as Dorothy said in the Wizard of Oz, "We are not in Kansas anymore, Toto!" The customs of these island people is vastly different from our own and you must take this into account as you deal with people in the Bahamas.

The first thing you will notice is attitude. There is always tomorrow. There are two kinds of time: Normal 24-hour daytime and island time. You are on island time now. If you think you want it done by tomorrow; think again. If a Bahamian says he will come to your boat and take care of something tomorrow, say to yourself, well that means probably this week. If he doesn't show up the next day, drop by and explain to him that you know that he was probably too busy to make it and does he now have an idea when he might make it. Don't be pushy and by all means don't expect it to be completed quickly, right the first time, or inexpensively. These things just don't happen on island time.

The main point of this is not to get worked up because things aren't done as quickly as you may want them. Go with the flow. Enjoy the quiet peacefulness of this island paradise. Remember, part of the reason you came here is for the adventure of exploring a new land and people. If it were just like the states, who would want to go?

Navigational Aids

The first channel you enter while in the Bahamas will quickly illustrate the inadequacy of navigational markers. Not only are markers few and far between, those that do exist are seldom the conventional markers you expect to see.

The charts show the first marker in Indian Cay Channel off West End as a red "2". Being new to the Bahamas you are probably expecting something like figure 1 in the picture to the right. In fact, in recent years it has looked like figure 2 in the picture to the right, if it was there at all.

Instead of a conventional day mark as you might expect, you will find a narrow wooden post with a board nailed across it down low. The board is shaped like an arrow and points to the left as you approach it from the open ocean. You pass this marker on your starboard. Instead of the eight day marks indicated on the charts, you will probably only find 3 posts all on the south side of the channel. You will probably never see a numbered day mark in any channel in the Abacos.

Navigational lights are just as bad. Even though the charts may indicate a light on a particularly important navigational aid, do not count on it. In one night crossing of the Little Bahama Bank I counted only one working navigational light out of the five I was supposed to see. I routinely see reports of "nearly half the lighthouses, lights and beacons are working". In the Bahamas you should not move at night unless you have the necessary experience to do so.

Let The Buyer Beware

There are no Walmarts in the Bahamas. Do not expect a generous refund policy anywhere in the islands. The rule is pretty much, if you bought it, you own it. Don't be under any illusion that if you buy a new radio in a box in a store and take it home only to find it doesn't work, that you will be able to return it for a refund or replacement. Not going to happen! Perhaps when you get back to the states you can get it repaired by the manufacturer under warranty. This will not happen in the Bahamas.

If you buy a dress, make sure you like it when you buy it. You are not going to get to return it. If you are buying some electronic item, have the salesperson plug it in and show you that it works before paying for it and leaving the store.

The idea of "no warranty and no guarantee" can best be illustrated by a story I tell about visiting a Kentucky Fried Chicken restaurant in the Abacos. I was standing in line. Ahead of me a gentlemen pointed out that the days special was 2 pieces of chicken, french fries and a medium soft drink for $4.95. He told the young lady behind the counter that he would have the special. He paid his $4.95. (No sales tax.)

In a couple of minutes she slid a tray to him containing two pieces of chicken and some french fries. He said, "Excuse me, where is the soft drink?"

A dolphin surfaced beside our anchored boat and remained there. He looked at us almost as if to say. "Why are you here?" Then, after about 3 minutes of holding himself almost stationary beside our boat, he left and we never saw him again.

She replied, "We don't have any today." He stared dumbfounded for a moment and then asked, "Well shouldn't you give me another piece of chicken or reduce the price if you have no soft drinks?" he asked. To which she replied, "That is not the special. The special is two pieces of chicken, french fires and a soft drink." In exasperation he said, "But you have no soft drinks!"

There was a moment of silence while the young woman stared at him like he was stupid. I nearly burst out laughing at his dilemma. Just at that moment, a man's head appeared from behind the counter. He was obviously on his knees working on the soft drink machine and trying to get it to function. He stated emphatically, "It's not my fault the soda machine is not working today!" Needless to say the man in front of me did not get any more chicken or a reduction in his price.

This situation just about sums up all your dealings with the Bahamian culture. There is no such axiom as "The customer is always right." Instead, it is that "The customer knows nothing, is extremely cunning and stupid and should be watched closely." There is no warranty or guarantee that any service provided will be right. You have no assurances that anything you buy will last or will work. In short, let the buyer beware.

If you receive inferior service at a particular store or booth, don't go back. If you don't like the meal at a particular restaurant, don't go back. Always inform your fellow boaters about your experience. It doesn't take long for word of mouth to alert everyone in the area about what to expect at a particular business. But, and this is most important, don't think any Bahamian businessman will care if you are unhappy. That particular facet of doing business has not spread throughout their culture as of yet. The most important thing to a Bahamian in business is that you don't blame them personally when the service expected and paid for is not received. Rather, it is to be expected, so it is not their fault.

Another problem you will encounter is that they do not like to admit they don't know something. Here is an example. You go into a hardware store looking for a common brown two-outlet receptacle and there are none on the shelf. They do have the ivory ones. You ask the manager when they might get some of the brown receptacles in. A typical response will be, "They don't make the brown ones anymore!" Not true, but since he/she doesn't have the foggiest idea when they might come in, this is the type response you will get. Simply thank the manager and go to another hardware store, either in that community or the next. Chances are they will have one in stock.

Money

The US dollar is used interchangeably throughout the Bahamas in conjunction with their own dollar. It is not uncommon to receive your change in both US and Bahamian currency. Many cruisers request US currency when receiving change in a transaction. Just one word of caution. Do not get too much Bahamian currency in your possession at one time. You would not want to get in a bind if the Bahamian currency was ever replaced or devalued. Also, while you can take it back to the states, some US banks will not exchange Bahamian money. Those that do will exchange only Bahamian paper currency, not change. So use it freely throughout the Bahamas, but as your trip draws to a close be sure to spend or exchange what Bahamian currency you have before returning to the states.

Getting money in the Bahamas is relatively easy. There are ATM's in Freeport, Nassau and Marsh Harbour. However, ATM's are scarce in the out-islands. Depending on your card issuer, you may have to pay a fee. When you are in one of the islands at some distance from Nassau, if the island community has a bank, you can use your credit card to get a cash advance, however, there is normally a fee for this service. Most merchants accept VISA/Mastercard and a few still add a service charge. It is best to ask first.

Taking your boat out for the day is one of those pleasures we all enjoy in the Abacos. However, don't plan on going alone. Your friends will want to come along. Ask the owners of Siris IV.

Also, if using a credit card to confirm a marina reservation, expect that your card will be charged at the time you make the reservation. Make certain you understand what the refund policy is if you have to cancel.

One final note on Bahamian banks. Banks in the larger communities like Georgetown, Marsh Harbour, Nassau and Freeport operate normal banking hours. However, very small branches may have very restricted hours. As an example the bank may be open only from 12 noon to 1 PM on Thursday. That is it. One day per week for one hour. So don't go to a small island bank and necessarily expect that they will be open Monday through Friday. It doesn't work that way.

Food

Small restaurants that provide meals are often referred to as "take aways". Here you can get a complete chicken dinner wrapped up in a container for about $7. The food is generally good and not too spicy. The local corner grocery usually offers food wrapped up in wax paper to be "eaten on the run". It is good and you should try some of the different items to see what they are like. These "fast food" meals are generally your best buy financially. In the larger communities like Marsh Harbour and Georgetown, someone will set up a food service out of the back of their car or van. Much like a "coach roach" might provide you at work in the states. These "cars" cater to the working Bahamian. Again the food is usually quite good and inexpensive.

If you plan to eat lunch at a regular tourist restaurant, plan on spending $8 to $10 for a hamburger and $12 for a chicken dinner. If you can find a local restaurant where the Bahamians eat, the price will be a little less.

Evening meals in restaurants are expensive. A chicken dinner may run $20 to $25 and steak $30. For this you get a baked potato, small salad, baked beans and the meat.

Our trawler is tied up against a concrete wall in one of the unfinished canal projects in the Abacos. This is Leisure Lee, one of the very secure class A harbors between Treasure Cay and Marsh Harbour. Only a 2-3 hour run from Marsh Harbour if a serious storm approaches.

On the smaller out islands, restaurants work on a totally different concept. They may serve meals only two or three nights a week. Each guest must sign up for and pay for the meal in advance. Thus if fish is being served on Wednesday night and you want some, you would go over sometime Wednesday and pay for your dinner and get a reservation in your name. In this situation, if asked, "Do you have a reservation?" they truly mean it. They literally cook only enough food for those that have ordered the meal. If you show up at dinnertime without a reservation, you probably will not get to eat. As you might expect, selection may be limited. The choice may be chicken or beef. Nothing else. These quaint restaurants provide good food, though expensive, and are a unique experience that you should try while in the Bahamas.

The fast food chains of the US are limited in the Bahamas. You will find them in Nassau and Freeport, but they make only very limited appearances in either Georgetown or Marsh Harbour, and nowhere else in the Bahamas.

Grocery stores in Marsh Harbour and Georgetown carry quite a large variety of food, though it is expensive. They are open seven days a week. Bananas, as well as most fruits and vegetables, are now readily available in most of the Bahamas. However, on the smaller out islands, stores may have a very limited selection and they may not be open on some days or during some periods you would expect them to be open. One more word of caution about grocery stores in the Bahamas. Normally they receive their stock of fresh vegetables and bread from the states one day each week. Say for example, Wednesday. If you go to the store on Tuesday you will find what is left of vegetables that have been picked over for a week. By going Wednesday morning you insure a good selection of fresh vegetables. Ask your fellow cruisers, they will know what day the food boat comes in that community.

It seems every island community has someone that runs a small bakery out of their home. Homemade bread, rolls, bread pudding, and cookies are easy to come by once you find out who makes them. This practice even continues when a grocery opens in the communities that carries these same baked products from the states. First, they usually are fresher and taste better, and finally, they are usually cheaper.

Each island community has someone that augments their income with fresh fish and garden vegetables. These people will come around with their wares and see if you are interested. It always seemed funny to me to have a little old lady knock on the stern of my boat and ask if I wanted fresh bananas, tomatoes, or conch. Whenever we bought it, it was always fresh and the price was usually quite good.

Your best source for good meals remains

Virtually every community in the Bahamas has a public dock. Here large supply vessels and commercial fishing vessels tie up to load and unload their cargo. You are not permitted to tie up your vessel and leave it there. Loading and unloading only, thank you.

your own stores from your own vessel. It is great fun to eat out occasionally, however it is pretty expensive and the selection is not always the best. For those of you concerned about your health, much of the food prepared locally is fried and not necessarily good for those on a low fat diet.

Mail

The mail system in the Bahamas works fairly well, although much slower than our standards. A letter or flat pack envelope sent first class through the US Postal Service to the Bahamas will arrive in about 6 to10 days. The cost is not excessive. Options for receiving mail include the US Postal Service, commercial mail services, UPS and FedEx. In November 2012 the U.S. Postal Service 1st Class International rate for a letter less than 1 oz. was $1.05. For 3 oz. it was $2.65. The rate for a large envelope (flat) was $3.23 for 3 oz. and $10.01 for 16 oz. Priority Mail and Express Mail is also available. Visit www.usps.com for details. FedEx also offer several options, the least expensive being FedEx International Economy. A package up to 16 oz. will cost $114.07 and arrive in 5-6 days. Their website is www.fedex.com/ratefinder.= UPS rates and delivery times are comparable. Note: It is recommended that you *do not* send important documents by regular mail.

Once you have settled on a mail service, the next issue is where do you have your mail sent. A lot depends on your situation while in the islands. If at anchor in a small community, go to the small post office (with limited hours) and ask them if you can have mail sent to you general delivery at that location. Also ask for the correct mailing address. Typically it will be something like this; Your Name, General Delivery, Man-O-War Cay, Abaco, Bahamas. By introducing yourself to the mail clerk (usually only one per island) that person gets to know you and there is not normally a problem getting your mail.

Another option is to have the mail sent to a marina where you are staying, or as in Georgetown, the local grocery. Check with the cruisers in the area where you are and they will point you in the right direction. Two important points. First, whenever mail is addressed insure it always includes the community and location (like state) in the Bahamas, not just the community.

As an example, there are two Great Guana Cays. If you don't specify either Abaco or Exuma, it may go to the wrong post office. The second point is don't count on rapid delivery. Ten days is the norm. I see it vary between 8 and 14 days on a regular basis. If it truly must be there by a specific date, you may want to go the expense of Federal Express, or USPS international express service. Over the years, the worst case of delivery took 42 days. It was over

the Christmas Holidays and there is no explanation of why it took so long. I assume the mail package got mixed in with some other Christmas packages and got lost in the shuffle. Four other packages of mail sent after that one actually arrived before it did. The worst case of non-delivery was two years. In November 1998 a package of mail was sent to us in the Bahamas at the same address we always used. It never did arrive in 1999 or 2000. In the fall of 2000 the package of mail was returned to the agency that handles our mail with no explanation. The envelope was addressed correctly. All the postage was on it. We have no idea to this day why it was never delivered.

The most important point is that we never totally lost a mail package, had anything removed from a mail package or lost any mail at all. The system works, although it is sometimes a little slower than we would like.

If anything is put in your mail package that feels like something other than mail, expect the

Golf carts are a popular mode of transportation in the Out Islands. The cart pictured above is located at Man-O-War Cay and is painted bright red with a water pump and hose on the rear deck. You guessed it! It is their fire truck.

mail package to be sidetracked to Bahamian Customs. The package will be opened and a duty could be added to the contents. You then receive a notice to report to the Post Office to pick up your package. Any duty will have to be paid at pick up. The Post Office employees have nothing to do with this. They simply collect the money specified by the Customs personnel. How can this impact you? Well a friend of mine sent me a cassette message instead of a letter. It delayed my mail package a week and cost me $2.52 to pick up the package.

Instruct your friends not to send you cassettes or VHS tapes, CD's or DVD's in the mail. Instruct the people that handle your mail to exclude anything but mail from your mail package. While you're at it you may want to tell those handling your mail in the states to hold on to all bulk rate mail until you return to the states. Paying first class to get a flyer from a store at home can be expensive, and you won't be able to take advantage of the sale anyway.

One final note on mail. You may want to send cards or letters to the US, Canada or Great Britain. Again the delivery is about 10 days by way of the Bahamian Postal System and costs about twice what US postage costs. However, cruisers frequently put US Postage on their letters and have them taken back to the states by one of the other cruisers who is flying back. That Good Samaritan then actually mails the letter once he or she gets to the US. Be sure to bring your own supply of US stamps. The Cruisers Net described later in this chapter handles this process. Mail Call cuts your cost and the time of delivery. If you are in an area of the Bahamas without an organized Cruisers Net, you will have to use Bahamian stamps and send the mail via the Bahamian Postal System.

Telephone

Card phones have replaced coin-operated public phones, and BTC (Bahamas Telecommunications Company, www.btcbahamas.com) cards are found throughout the Bahamas. These cards are preloaded with a specific amount of money ($5, $10, $20) and work for local and international calls. For calls within the Bahamas, seven digit dialing is used within an island group, and a prefix of 1-242 is used for calls to other island groups. International calls are expensive and some 800 calls are not toll free. International Direct Dial phone, where available, accept credit cards. Increasingly, locals use cell phones. Cellular service is available, however, you must first register with BTC. If your service provider does not have an agreement with BTC, you will need a SIM card from BTC to use your phone. The phone must be unlocked and dual band, not tri-band. You can buy an inexpensive phone that meets these requirements in the U.S. Prepaid cell phone cards are available in various amounts up to $100.00. The per minute rate varies by time of day. The least expensive time is 7 p.m. to 7 a.m. with incoming call at $0.15 per minute and outgoing at $0.44 per minute. You can significantly reduce your per minute charges by using a call back system such as Globaltel. Visit their website, www.globaltel-callback.com for details. Another options for cell phone use is to rent a unit from BTC. And finally, there is the options of using Skype VOIP when an internet connection is available.

E-Mail/Internet

Internet service is available through in many areas of the Bahamas. Rates and type of service varies. Batelco, the government owned phone company, operates a service called Batelnet. Their website is www.batelnet.bs. Out Island Internet (OII) operates in the Abacos and now offers high speed wireless. Their website is www.acacoinet.com. Both sites will provide you with information about service and pricing options.

Most marinas now offer some type of internet service, either free or for a fee. Often it is wireless. Several businesses offer access for patrons. If you are anchoring, a good range extender may get you on line through an unsecured site, sometime residential.

Cruisers report that no matter who the service is through, all providers have server problems. There are frequent outages, sometimes lasting for extended periods of time. Bottom line, internet is available, just not at the level of quality you expect at home.

News

Newspapers are available in many communities and several are on-line. A sampling includes the Nassau Gaurdian, Freeport News, Abaconian, and The Bahama Journal.

There are a number of local radio stations, but the news tends to be very local in nature and it is hard to get good international coverage or coverage of the states. The one TV station in Nassau has some very limited local news and broadcasts. In the Abacos you can listen to FM 93.5 out of Marsh Harbour for local news and weather.

Satellite TV is your best bet for news, and if you don't have that, many marinas now offer cable TV service.

Sea Beans

A popular past time in the Bahamas is walking the ocean beaches examining the flotsam and jetsam that washes ashore. Among the flotsam are Sea Beans, also referred to as drift seeds. These Sea Beans are seedpods that have fallen from trees or vines in places such as Africa and South America and have drifted in the ocean currents, finally arriving on beaches in the Bahamas.

The most familiar drift seed is the coconut, but there are a wide variety of drift seeds in various shapes and sizes. Two types often found in the Bahamas are the "Heart Beans" (shown at the right) and the "Hamburger Bean". The Heart Bean is a large brown bean, heart shaped, flat and about 2 inches across. The Heart Bean can be sanded and polished to a high luster. The Hamburger Bean, as its name implies, looks like a miniature

hamburger. It is round, with the top and bottom a light tan color. Around the middle is a dark stripe that makes it look like a hamburger patty in a bun. There are several variations of the Hamburger Bean, but they are all about the size of a nickel. For more information about Sea Beans, go to the Website, www.seabean.com.

A heart shaped Sea Bean found on the beaches in Abaco by the crew of Kokopelli.

Laundry

For those not using on board equipment, many marinas offer token operated washers and dryers. You can expect to pay from $3 to $6 per load to wash, and the same to dry. In some areas laundry services are available and for $12 you can have a load washed, dried and folded.

Liquor

Beer, wine and alcohol are readily available in most communities throughout the Bahamas. The one exception I know of is Man-O-War Cay in the Abacos. Man-O-War is a religious community and the sale of alcohol and tobacco are not permitted.

Where available, beer is expensive at about $40 or more per case, while wine and alcohol are very reasonable, often cheaper than the same product would cost in the states.

Cruisers Net

VHF: Cruisers pass information on local VHF nets in the areas where many gather: Nassau, Marsh Harbour and Georgetown. These networks are run by locals and cruisers and follow a similar format. In Marsh Harbour, the net begins at 8:15am with the weather, followed by headline news, sports, community news, local merchant announcements, OPEN MIKE, which is for cruisers to make any appropriate comments, and finally arrival and departures.

SSB: There is an informal net, the Cruiseheimer's Net, for the entire east coast at 8:30am on SSB 8152. There are announcements of interest and cruisers check in from various locations. Traffic is passed through a net controller. Chris Parker operates the Caribbean Weather Network and transmits on SSB 4045 at 6:30am and 8 am and again at 9:30 am on SSB 12359.

Trash Disposal

Trash disposal is a real concern while cruising in the Bahamas. Number 1, do not just throw your waste overboard and number 2, don't take it ashore on uninhabited islands and leave it there in bags. The birds and animals will open the bags and soon the trash is everywhere.

It is a sad situation that most of us go to the Bahamas to enjoy the beautiful beaches and clean clear water only to have it ruined by the same people who came to enjoy it. Already a lot of trash has been dumped by visiting boaters all over the Bahamas. On almost any island where you stop, you will find bags of garbage left by insensitive and uncaring boaters. Don't be one of the them!

A narrow roadway in the Bahamas. Wide enough for a golf cart.

Trash disposal is limited to islands with communities. Expect to pay $2 or $3 a bag to dispose of trash at the smaller communities. Only in the larger communities are there normally free trash disposal points.

Collect your trash in heavy black plastic bags. Crush all trash to reduce the size. Biodegradable food waste can be thrown overboard in remote areas, but not harbors. Cans, bottles, paper, etc should all be bagged together. Find a place to store the full bags when cruising in the more remote areas.

Bicycles and Scooters

Many cruisers carry either bicycles or motor scooters on board. On the large islands with communities, there are small narrow roads where you can ride your vehicle. Only on the larger islands are the roads wide enough for a full sized car. On the smaller islands the "roads" may more closely resemble golf cart paths, as you would see them on a golf course. In fact golf carts are a popular means of transportation on some of the islands.

While bicycles do not require insurance, motorized vehicles must be insured. Bahamian insurance is easy to obtain in any large city, such as Marsh Harbor. First you present a valid drivers license, cruising permit and vehicle's title to one of the many insurance companies. In minutes you will have your policy, stickers, and forms for the vehicle at surprisingly reasonable rates. Then you must make a quick stop at the police department to get a Bahamian plate, which expires on your next birthday. Please note, helmets are mandatory by Bahamian law. A quick way to get a ticket in the Bahamas is to ride a scooter/motorcycle without a helmet.

Routine Maintenance

You should perform the routine maintenance on your vessel according to your normal schedule. Used engine oil is a little more difficult to dispose of the in Bahamas and you may have to carry it with you in containers until you reach a community where you can dispose of it.

Zincs appear to deteriorate quicker in the warm Bahamian waters. Plan on replacing them more often. Some cruisers extend the life of their zincs by attaching an additional zinc on an electric line and lowering it into the water beside their vessel. This additional zinc must be grounded to your vessel ground system to help prolong the life of your regular zincs.

Marine growth begins to appear on the best bottom paint after about 30-45 days in the warm waters of the Bahamas. Plan on "scrubbing" the bottom of your vessel about once per month to rid it of the growth and to refresh the bottom paint. Barnacles do not seem to be much of a problem for vessels with a good bottom paint job.

A photo taken while cleaning the bottom of our trawler. Scrubbing the bottom to "freshen" the paint should be accomplished every 30-45 days.

Dinghies left in the water for prolonged periods also begin to develop a growth on their bottom. The easiest way to get rid of it is to turn your dinghy up side down on a beach and pour vinegar on the affected area. Wait about 30 minutes and most of the growth will come right off with a little scrubbing.

Marine heads are affected by the salt water and urine. A hard crystal forms inside the head bowl and in the discharge hoses. To reduce this problem, give your head "salad oil" about once per week. Make a mixture of ½ oil and ½ vinegar. Pour it into your head and let it work down to the overboard seacock. Close the seacock over night and let everything in the system soak in the "salad oil mixture". Open the seacock and flush completely the next day. This mixture will help keep your system clean, reduce odors and lubricate your head's working parts.

Chapter 6
The Abacos

The last two chapters of this book are dedicated to providing information on the two most popular destinations in the Bahamas, the Abacos and Exumas. If you are a first time visitor to the Bahamas, I hope your plan is to visit the Abacos first. If you are going to the Abacos, you should have acquired the following charts and cruising guides while outfitting for the Bahamas.

- **Waterway Guide, Bahamas 2013 Edition**
- **NV-Charts Chartbook Region 9.1 or**
- **Explorer Chartbook Near Bahamas,** by Monty & Sara Lewis
- **The Cruising Guide to Abaco Bahamas,** by Steve Dodge
- **Great Abaco and Cays Chart, AB001,** (Optional)

When visiting the Abacos, your most likely departure point is Lake Worth. Your landfall should be West End, Grand Bahama Island, although some people choose Memory Rock. Those that make landfall at West End can clear customs there and then can travel freely about the Bahamas as they wish as they make their way east to Marsh Harbour. Those that bypass West End should proceed straight across the north end of the Little Bahama Bank to Spanish Cay or Green Turtle Cay and clear customs.

I recommend that everyone clear customs in West End. The law requires you to proceed to the nearest port of entry when you enter a foreign country. While it is true that people go all the way across the Little Bahama Bank and clear customs in Marsh Harbour, those that do are in violation of the customs and immigration law. If your vessel were to be stopped by the Bahamian National Defense force while at anchor in Great Sale Cay or somewhere else you would be hard pressed to explain why you did not stop at Walkers Cay to the north or West End to the south when you entered their country. The result could be serious fines or, at the very least, a paperwork nightmare.

The Dodge and Waterway cruising guides recommended above provide excellent waypoint information, local phone numbers, layout of communities and everything else you might want to know about the Abacos. With either in hand you can safely explore the Abacos and enjoy your first time cruise there. During the remainder of this chapter, I will simply point out some of the highlights of the Abacos for those reading this book that do not yet have one of the other guides.

Refer to the maps on the previous two pages as you proceed through the rest of this chapter. This drawing shows the location and relationship of all the most important Cays (Pronounced Keys) in the Abacos.

West End

At one time West End was a very busy community. The Jack Tar Resort was located there and literally thousands of people came and went each month. With more than 5 hotels, a large entertainment center, golf course, private airport, commercial dock, marina, etc. West End had everything including a fair sized community just outside the gate to the Jack Tar Resort. When gambling casinos were permitted in Lucaya and not West End, it was the end for the Jack Tar Resort. In a few short years it fell into disrepair like so many other projects in the Bahamas.

In 1998 a new group bought the land at West End and demolished the old Jack Tar Resort. They renovated the Jack Tar Marina and renamed it the Old Bahama Bay Marina. Additional plans called for a mega-development to include shops, a hotel/resort and condos. While the residential and retail plans continue to struggle, The Old Bahama Bay Resort and Yacht Harbour offers a gated, five-star resort with transient dockage and many amenities in a very protected harbor. This is a class A harbor (See appendix C) with one marina and no anchorage and no mooring balls. You can clear customs there, call home to let your loved ones know you made it across the Gulf Stream and, if necessary, wait in a very protected marina for good weather to finish your journey across the Little Bahama Bank to Marsh Harbour, Abacos.

Freeport/Port Lucaya

East of West End about 20 miles along the south shore of the Grand Bahama Island is the second largest city in the Bahamas, Freeport. Be sure to stay off shore 2-3 miles as a reef runs all along the southern shore of Grand Bahama Island. You normally do not enter the Freeport commercial harbor with your pleasure craft. About five miles east of the Freeport Harbor entrance you come to a relatively narrow channel leading to Xanadu Beach Marina in a Class A harbor. **Note:** At publication the resort website states the property is for sale). Farther east a short distance is the entrance channel to the Ocean Reef Yacht Club at N26° 29.22 and W78° 39.50. This club provides a very protected basin in a Class A harbor with easy access to Freeport. **Note:** This is not a port of entry. The next channel is Bell Channel where you enter the Class A harbor of Port Lucaya. Two large marinas and a small anchorage are available, but no mooring balls. The marinas are Grand Bahama Yacht Club. This is the busiest of all marinas in Freeport and Port Lucaya and is a port of entry. Port Lucayan Marina is a state of the art facility and a port of entry.

Our trawler and a buddy boat tied up in the Grand Lucayan Canal waiting out weather. Hard to believe, the wind is blowing NW30-35 knots. What a great class A harbor.

Transportation to the bustling city of Freeport is readily available via either taxi or bus. The casinos and tourist shops are the major attraction here, although there is a nice beach along the south shore. Most cruisers quickly tire of Freeport/Lucaya and are anxious to keep moving east.

Freeport is fact one of the few places in the Bahamas where you can have major work done on your vessel. Inside the commercial harbor of Freeport in the fourth basin on the right is Bradford Marine Bahamas, a full service marine yard. With docking accommodations for those wanting work done, this first class facility is equipped to provide just about any maintenance you might want whether your boat is 32' long or 200' long. Trained diesel mechanics are on staff. Call 242-352-7711, FAX 242-352-7695, E-Mail info@bradfordmarinebahamas.com or visit their web site at www.bradfordmarinebahamas.com.

Grand Lucayan Waterway

Five miles east of the Bell Channel into Lucaya is the entrance to the Grand Lucayan waterway. This 7 mile long waterway cuts the Grand Bahama Island in half. 8' deep and 250 feet wide this canal has concrete lined walls for most of its entire length. Finished in the 1970s this Fort Lauderdale style community of the Bahamas went from being a spectacular success to a total failure overnight when the new independent Bahamian Government ruled that foreigners could not own land in the Bahamas. The 5,000 lots already sold to people in the US and Britain were in limbo.

As a result of this legal battle homes were never built on the many cul-de-sacs already laid out on the canal, and the land became overgrown with weeds. Although now resolved, very few homes have yet to be built and the Grand Lucayan Waterway is largely uninhabited. This is a class A harbor and anchorage with ample room for vessels to tie up overnight on the abandoned concrete walls. The Grand Lucayan Canal makes an excellent hurricane harbor or harbor of refuge on the Grand Bahama Island.

There is a fixed 27.5' bridge spanning the canal that prevents sailboats from traversing the length of the canal. However, there is room on either end for sailboats to enter and seek refuge. The south end offers a deep well protected entrance off the Northwest Passage. The north end of the canal only provides 3.5' MLW and should be traversed only on a half tide rising by deeper draft vessels. Both ends of the canal are exceptional well marked by Bahamian standards.

Memory Rock

Memory Rock is a small rock jutting out of the surface on the western edge of the Little Bahama Bank. Vessels that choose to come onto the Little Bahama Bank via the Memory Rock route may pass to either side of the rock and take a heading for Mangrove Cay. Some vessels anchor on the bank a few miles in from the banks edge waiting for good weather to return to the states. This is a class G anchorage only with no marina or mooring balls. Make certain you avoid the charted shoal to the north.

Mangrove Cay

This small cay is where all three routes along the northern half of the Little Bahamas Bank meet. It is routine to see several sailboats anchored in the lee of this small island. There is nothing ashore, although a small plane wreck on the southern shore is interesting to explore. This is class F anchorage with no marina or mooring balls.

Great Sale Cay

Great Sale Cay is by far the most popular anchorage on the Little Bahama Bank. The uninhabited island provides a place to go

Deserted wind swept beaches are plentiful on the islands of the northern Abacos.

ashore. There is nothing on the island but brush. This is a class B anchorage with no mooring balls or marina. On most nights during the winter cruising season there are 5-10 boats at anchor here. Some vessels make this their first stop when coming from the states and their last stop before crossing back.

Walkers Cay

On the northern edge of the Little Bahamas Bank is the outpost of the Abacos. Walkers Cay is very small and Walkers Cay Marina is now closed. This is a class A harbor but does not provide an anchorage or mooring balls. There is an airfield and you can clear customs as a customs officer and immigration officer are in residence.

Grand Cay

A group of islands on the northern edge of the bank, consisting of Grand, Big Grand, Little Grand, Mermaid, Rat, and Felix Cay just to mention the major ones. A small community there provides the basic needs including some small stores and restaurants. The Class C anchorage between Little Grand and Rat Cay provides easy access to Grand Cay. Rosie's Place, (call sign "Love Train" on VHF 68) a 15 slip marina, is located in Grand Cay.

Double Breasted, Strangers, and Carters Cays

Small-uninhabited cays along the northern Little Bahama Bank. No marinas, mooring balls or services on any of them. All offer fine beaches and fun places to go ashore, but rates only Class D for anchorage.

Fox Town and Hawksbill Cay

In the center of the northern shore of the Little Abaco Island is Fox Town located in the protection of Hawksbill Cay. While there is no marina or mooring balls there, there is a protected anchorage and some limited services if you dinghy ashore to Fox Town. This is a very poor small community. The anchorage is rated Class C.

Allans-Pensacola Cay

These uninhabited cays became one in a hurricane and offer a Class C harbor with poor holding, no marina and no mooring balls. There is an abandoned Missile Tracking station on the island, but little else except deserted beaches and heavy underbrush. A shallow Class A keyhole harbor exists on the southern end of this island. The entrance channel only provides 3' MLW, with no easy access to shore and a lot of bugs. Don't plan on using this harbor without charts, and only if a strong storm is coming your way.

Spanish Cay

This small privately owned island offers Spanish Cay Marina in a class B manmade harbor on the southern end and a class natural B harbor on the northern end. There are no mooring balls. As the island is a controlled community, you are not permitted to go ashore here. If you are staying in the marina, you are welcome to walk around the island.

Powell Cay and Coopers Town

Powell Cay offers pristine beauty and a nice class F anchorage, as well as the remains for a number of sunken boats. Opposite Powell Cay on Great Abaco Island is the small community of Coopers Town. There are a few grocery stores and restaurants, plus Esso and Shell fuel docks. In the event of an emergency, there is a small hospital here.

Manjack Cay

Often referred to as Munjack Cay. This island has a few houses on it but boaters still have beach access to the beach which offers great shelling. There is also a nature trail in the mangrove swamp. Bring bug spray. The anchorage on the south side is class C with no marina or mooring balls.

The area shown to the right is referred to as the "Hub of the Abacos". A description of important points in the "Hub" is given during the rest of this chapter starting on the pages that follow.

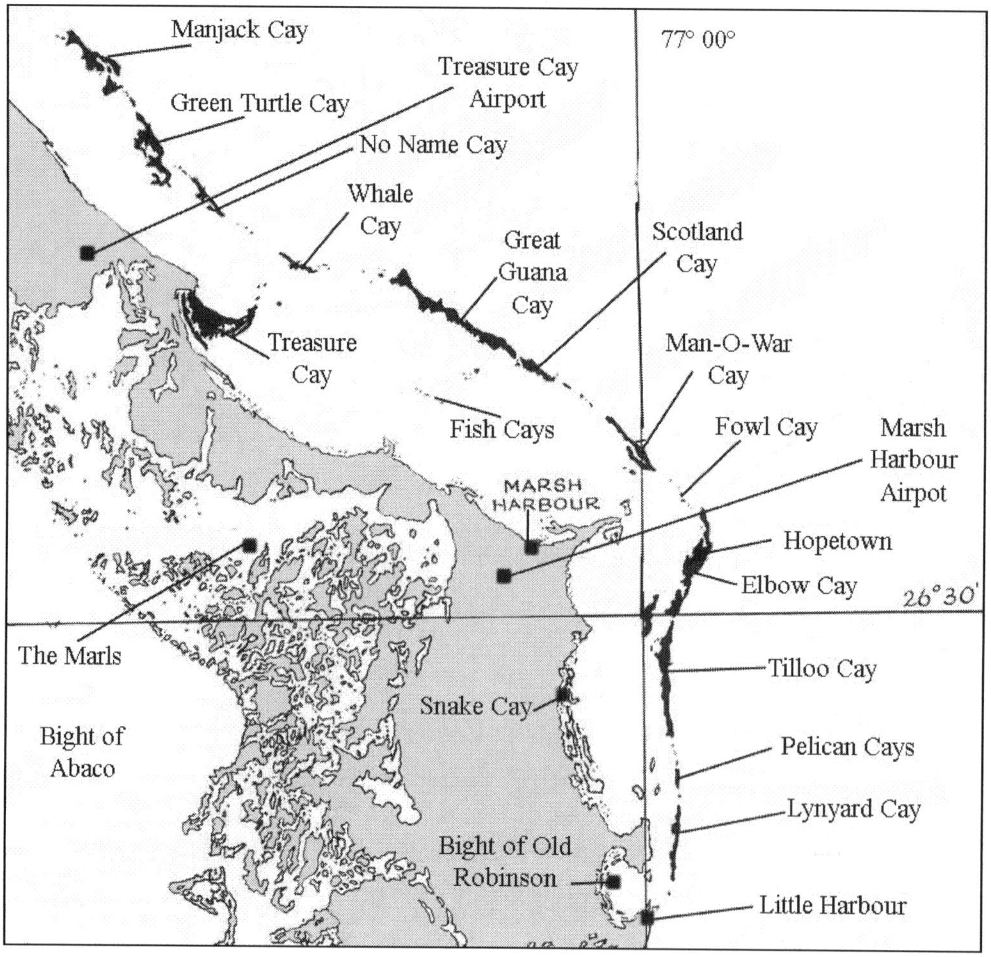

Green Turtle Cay

One of the more popular stops in the Abacos. Green Turtle Cay boasts not one, but two Class A harbors with marinas, mooring balls and anchorages. Both entrance channels are restricted to 4 ½' MLW. Mooring balls in the northern harbor (White Sound) and in the southern (Black Sound) are available for a small fee. The northern harbor has two marinas, Bluff House and Green Turtle Club Marinas. The southern harbor also has two marinas, Black Sound Marina and The Other Shore Club, and the Abaco Yacht Services boat yard. In addition, the fair sized community of New Plymouth provides restaurants, gift shops, two hardware stores, bank, post office, and two groceries. Many deep draft sailboats anchor off the western shore of the island near the town of New Plymouth and this is rated only a class D anchorage with no mooring balls or marina.

The streets are often narrow in the small villages in the Out Islands. On the main street of New Plymouth, Green Turtle Cay, Abaco, there is just enough room for two golf carts to pass.

The southern harbor, Black Sound, offers one of the few places in the Bahamas where large pleasure craft can be hauled and stored in a boat yard. Abaco Yacht Services operates a full service boat yard with 30-ton lift. Phone 242-365-4033, Fax 242-365-4216, Email ays@oii.net or visit ays@oii.net.

Of particular interest to many cruisers are the Coral Reef Mooring Buoys placed on the ocean side of Manjack (Munjack) and Green Turtle Cays. A series of 18 buoys have been installed by the Reef Relief Organization with the support of the Green Turtle Cay Foundation. Mooring balls are numbered 1 to 18 starting with 1 (Munjack North) to 18 (Catacombs) in the south. Mooring balls are available on a first come, first serve basis. There is no charge for their use. Check out the information on these mooring balls at www.reefrelieffounders.com/bahamas-reef-mooring-program. On the website you can print out a map of all mooring ball locations at Green Turtle Cay.

Treasure Cay

Treasure Cay was built as a planned resort and now boasts a Class A harbor with Treasure Cay Hotel Resort and Marina, an anchorage and mooring balls. Located on the Great Abaco Island SW of Green Turtle Cay, Treasure Cay has a small grocery, post office, car rental, golf cart rental, tennis courts, golf course, and a world-class beach. Mooring balls available for $12/day and anchoring is $10/day. The fee includes the use of showers and facilities. There are numerous cottages to rent and an airport. The beach is reportedly one of the 10 most beautiful in the word and should not be missed.

Whale Cay

The uninhabited island of Whale Cay is located between Green Turtle Cay and Great Guana Cay on the very edge of the bank. This cay is well known because most boaters must go off the bank and around this cay in the open ocean to get to the southern portion of the Abacos. This is made necessary by the fact that the bank has silted in so much behind Whale Cay that most deep draft vessels cannot pass between Whale Cay and the Great Abaco Island. The cruising guide provides two channels for shoal draft vessels behind Whale Cay, but both must be taken in fair weather. The ocean sends substantial rollers into the channel at both ends of Whale Cay and the Whale Cay passage is one of the areas you must be concerned about a "rage" occurring (See chapter 2). For an update, ask for Whale Cay passage reports on VHF 16.

Great Guana Cay

This island boasts a very small neat community complete with hardware store, village grocery, school, post office, phone company and two resorts. There are two harbors of interest on Great Guana. On the north west edge is Baker's Bay. Here are the remains of yet another failed venture in the Bahamas. A cruise ship line developed this pristine bay as a destination complete with deep-water channel. When it did not work out, they just walked away and left everything where it was. Today the island created (Shell Island) by the channel dredging provides an interesting spot to hunt for shells while the beach at Baker's Bay is first class. There will often be 5-10 boats at anchor in the class C harbor there.

This is also the location of Baker's Bay Golf and Ocean Club, a large private resort. Transient dockage is available. Unfortunately this eliminates portions of the anchorage and the beach walks.

Midway down the island on the west side is the community harbor for Great Guana Cay. This class C harbor has a marina, mooring balls and anchoring. Mooring balls are available for a fee. Orchid Bay Marina has recently reinforced their breakwater across a good part of the harbor opening. This makes this an even better protected harbor (Class B), however it can still be uncomfortable when winds are from the west or northwest.

No discussion of Great Guana Cay would be complete without mentioning Nippers. This restaurant and bar on top of the ocean side of

Nippers provides free gulf cart rides to the restaurant, a great view of the ocean, a first class beach, great reef swimming, a bar with swimming pool and wonderful food.

the island provides a breath taking view of the ocean and reef, as well as good food, drink, and music. Nippers is known for its swimming pool within the bar area and the Pig Roast buffet every Sunday also the annual Barefoot Man Concert scheduled for the first Sunday of March each year.

Man-O-War Cay

Man-O-War Cay boasts a clean industrious community of descendants from Loyalists that are strongly supported by their faith. Long a community that built boats, today that tradition continues and both fiberglass fishing boats and small wooden dinghies are built there. Man-O-War offers two class A harbors. In the northern harbor in front of the village is Man-O-War Marina, a boat yard, mooring balls and an anchorage. Mooring balls are available for a fee. The southern harbor (Called Eastern Harbour) offers mooring balls and anchoring.

Entrance to both harbors is gained by a narrow channel near the southwest end of the island that carries 5' MLW. Just about any type repair on a vessel can be made in Man-O-War Cay and the boat yard provides steady employment for a number of locals. There are two groceries, one restaurant, a hardware store, bank, and a number of tourist gift shops, including the Sail Shop. This is a unique shop were bags and other items are sewn on-site.

Marsh Harbour

Opposite Man-O-War Cay on the Great Abaco Island is Marsh Harbour, the largest community in the Abacos. There is a class B harbor there replete with mooring balls, 5 marinas and room for 100 boats to anchor. The harbor will support vessels with a 6' draft. Presently open are the Marsh Harbour Marina, Conch Inn Resort & Marina, Boat Harbour, Harbour View Marina and Mangoes Marina. Abaco Beach Resort is outside the harbor.

The community has two shopping centers, several well stocked grocery stores, liquor stores, hardware stores, laundromats, many fine restaurants, motel and hotel space, and tourist gift shops. On the edge of town is the largest airport in the Abacos, a place to fill propane tanks, and a nursery and garden store.

The Marsh Harbour Boat Yard has an 85-ton lift and is a full service yard. Telephone is 242-367-5205, Fax 242-367-4018, Email info@mhby.com or

The Hope Town lighthouse is reputed to be the most photographed lighthouse in the Bahamas.

visit the website at www.mhby.com. The yard also provides long term storage. This boat yard is located outside the Marsh Harbour harbor area along the southeast shore of Abaco Island about a 1 mile walk from the Conch Marina.

On any given night cruisers can be found in any of the many restaurants and bars enjoying the nightlife and having a good time. There are always organized activities going on and the Cruisers Net is very active here. The Royal Marsh Harbour Yacht Club provides monthly social meetings with food and drink for all members. Membership is open to all cruisers. In addition the RMHYC sponsors a radio net on VHF Channel 78 on Monday, Wednesday and Fridays mornings at 8AM. Members are brought up to date on club happenings, new members, arrivals and departures, and who might take mail back to the US, Canada or UK.

Membership also entitles you to fly their burgee and provides you with a sanctioned yacht club membership card that is now recognized in some stateside yacht clubs. Be sure to check into membership if you will be in the area for a couple of months, plan to return on a regular basis, or feel you may be able to use the card in some yacht clubs. I have used mine on a regular basis on the Great Lakes. You can check out the Royal Marsh Harbour Yacht Club at www.RMHYC.com.

Hope Town (Elbow Cay)

The community of Hope Town on Elbow Cay is located east of Marsh Harbour. Hope Town has a Class A harbor complete with three marinas, Lighthouse Marina, Hopetown Hideaways and Marina, and Hope Town Inn and Marina. There are many mooring balls and limited anchorage space. Mooring balls are available for a fee. The town surrounds the harbor and has restaurants, grocery, gift shops, post office, phone office, and the best-known lighthouse in the Abacos.

The lighthouse at Hope Town is frequently photographed, still operates today with 1800 technology, and is open to the public.

The harbor entrance will carry 5'MLW.

Further south on Elbow Cay is White Sound, and Sea Spray Marina. There are no mooring balls. Tahiti Beach is a popular shelling spot. You can also tie up at the Abaco Inn dinghy dock to enjoy a great meal with a marvelous view of the ocean.

Little Harbour

Little Harbour boasts the last well protected harbor as you head south about 15 miles from Marsh Harbour. Beyond Little Harbour the cruiser must go out onto the ocean. Little Harbour is the normal jumping off point for vessels sailing south from the Abacos to Nassau, Eleuthera or the Exumas.

Little Harbour offers a class A harbor with mooring balls (fee), room for 10 vessels to anchor and very limited marina space.

The communities' primary claim to fame is its founder Randolph Johnston who settled there in the 1950s. He was an internationally known artist and he built a forge, studio, and a bar. After Randolph passed in 1992 his son Pete has built up the trade at Pete's Pub and it is well known in the boating community. There are no other services there, except the pub. One can tour the forge and studio.

Off to the northwest from Little Harbour is an area called the Bight of Old Robinson. This area's claim to fame is the blue holes. Blue holes are so called because from the air they look like a blue hole in the middle of the white sand. These holes are actually the entrance to a cave

This 4' wide bronze turtle is mounted on a stake in Little Harbor, Abacos. Home of the famous sculpture, Randolph Johnson, this bronze is one of his works.

that connects with the sea via a long twisting cavern. The tide rushes in and out of these holes twice each day and they are very deep. Divers should approach them with great caution as the current can drag you in and you will probably drown long before you reach the ocean. Several years ago some young boys were lost in one of the blue holes in the Bight of Old Robinson. Their parents erected a monument in their memory at the entrance to this blue hole.

Summary

We have tried to provide you with some information to assist you in traveling to and around the Abacos. Much more detailed information is available in the cruising guide by Steve Dodge and in the Waterway Guide, Bahamas 2013 edition.

The area west of the Great Abaco Island is largely uninhabited and uncharted. This area is referred to as the Bight of Abaco and the cruising information available is very limited.

Chapter 7
The Exumas

In route to the Exumas you must pass over the Great Bahama Bank and proceed to Nassau. The first part of this chapter deals with that trip. While outfitting for a trip to the Exumas you should have acquired the following cruising guides and charts.

- **Waterway Guide, Bahamas 2013 Edition**
- **NV-Charts Chartbook Region 9.2 or**
- **Explorer Chartbook Near Bahamas,** by Monty & Sara Lewis

In crossing to the Great Bahama Bank, your most likely departure point is Ft. Lauderdale, Miami or a point just south in the Florida Keys. Your initial destination should be Bimini or Cat Cay. Refer to the drawing below as you proceed through the first part of this trip to Nassau.

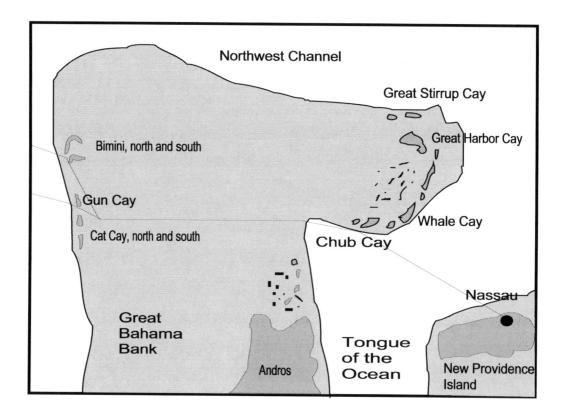

I prefer to make landfall and clear customs at Bimini. Bimini provides more exposure to the Bahamian culture than Cat Cay. Use the waypoint on the recommended chart and follow the instructions in the cruising guide closely as you enter the channel between North and South Bimini. The channel carries 5'MLW.

Bimini

The principle community on North Bimini is Alice Town. The harbor at Alice Town is a class D harbor (See appendix C) with 5 marinas and a fair anchorage just past the last marina. The moorings placed in the harbor have not been maintained and are no longer available for rent. If you choose to anchor here two anchors, in a Bahamian moor, are advisable as the tide rushes through the harbor. The bottom has a thin layer of sand which is difficult to penetrate. The five marinas are Sea Crest Marina, Weech's Bimini Dock, Bimini Big Game Marina, Bimini Blue Water Resort, Bimini Sandst and Brown's Marina.

Alice Town is easily explored by foot and consists of several shops and restaurants. A new channel has been dredged in the harbor northward to the Bimini Bay area where the Bimini Bay Resort and Marina is located. Further development will include a residential complex, casino and golf course.

A word of **caution**. The entrance to the harbor should not be attempted in strong wind conditions. Serious shoaling is reported in the former entrance channel, and a new channel has been dredged. If you are the least bit uncertain, call one of the marinas for guidance.

Cat Cay

The harbor at Cat Cay is manmade. The entrance to the bank is actually between Gun Cay to the north and North Cat Cay to the south. North Cat Cay is a privately owned island with the Cat Cay Yacht Club. Vessels are permitted to tie up there for a fee and clear customs. The fee for short-term tie up is waived if you pay to stay the night in the marina. However, there is nothing on the island except the club. The club provides a class B harbor with marina only. Both north and south of North Cat Cay are uninhabited islands. Gun Cay has an attractive fair weather class F harbor where vessels can wait to cross to Chub Cay. There is a nice beach.

A small public dock at low tide. Often found on small islands.

The Berry Islands

This is a good time to remind you that you should not depend on the navigation lights and/or day marks shown on the charts. As often as not, the two day marks in route to Chub Cay, Russell Light and the Northwest Channel buoy light, are out or missing all together.

From Cat Cay most vessels head east towards Chub Cay and on to Nassau. We have diverted NE to Great Harbour Cay in strong east winds to avoid going out on the Tongue of the Ocean with its 10' waves. Great Harbour Cay provides a class A harbor with the Great Harbour Cay Marina and an anchorage. The entrance to Great Harbour Cay is just south of Bullocks Harbour and is through a narrow manmade cut. Bullocks Harbour is the only settlement in the Berry Islands and offers some supplies and fresh items, a clinic, post office and various restaurants and bars.

North of Great Harbour Cay is Great Stirrup Cay. Great Stirrup provides two class C harbors with anchorages in Slaughter Harbour and Panton Cove. This can be a fair place to wait out north winds before heading south down the east side of the Berry Islands. Great Stirrup Cay is uninhabited.

Midway down the east side of the Berry Islands is Little Harbour Cay. Little Harbour Cay provides a class B harbor with anchorage for a couple of boats. There is a house on the island and a caretaker. The house is usually closed, but the caretaker is always there. There is good fishing and ample conch to be caught in the harbor. This is a safe place to wait for that good day to shoot across the 36 miles to Nassau.

The normal stop for most vessels in the Berry Islands is Chub Cay. Joined to Frazers Hog Cay at the hip, there is a full service marina, Chub Cay Marina, located in a class A harbor here. Anchorages are available west of Chub Cay and east of Frazers Hog Cay. Both would only be rated class D. Chub Cay is host to a private club although transients are welcome. There is an airfield and customs office, but not much else for the transient vessel. There is also a marina, Berry Island Club, on the east side of Frazer Hog Cay but it only provides class F protection.

New Providence Island
Nassau

Nassau, the capitol of the Bahamas, is located on the northeast corner of New Providence Island at the edge of the Tongue of the Ocean. It boasts a large protected class C harbor that caters to large cruise ships, ocean going freighters and small pleasure craft as well. The constant coming and going of vessels combined with wind and current insure that your stay in the harbor will not be a calm one.

Be sure to follow the instructions in the cruising guide on entering the harbor in Nassau.

The city does offer everything you might want in a large city, including post office, banks, supermarkets, hardware stores, restaurants, tourist shops, etc. There is also a very interesting historical fort, Fort Fincastle, overlooking the harbor that is well worth a visit. Across the bridge to the ocean side is Paradise Island with its interesting and expensive night` life of casinos and shown.

Changing of the guard in Nassau.

There are five marinas in the harbor and room to anchor if you work at it. However, this is a very busy harbor with extensive boat traffic and large cruise ships coming and going and it thus can be very uncomfortable. In addition, no matter where you anchor, security will be an issue. Many cruisers make sure they are back on their boats by dark.

Keep things locked, be aware of you environment and practice the neighborhood watch system.

The Marina at Atlantis and Hurricane Hole Marina offer good protection against wakes. Nassau Yacht Haven, Nassau Harbour Club, and Bayshore Marina offer adequate, but less, wake protection.

If headed south to the Exumas and you have been some time getting to Nassau, you may want to top off your water and fuel tanks and food supplies. It will only get more expensive as you go further south.

Finally, if you plan to clear customs here you will have to do it at a marina.

The Exumas

Before leaving Nassau for the Exumas you should have the following cruising guide and chart book on board:

- **Waterway Guide, Bahamas 2013 Edition**
- **The Exuma Guide,** by Stephen Pavlidis
- **NV Charts- Chartbook Region 9.2 or**
- **Explorer Chartbook Exumas,** By Monty and Sara Lewis

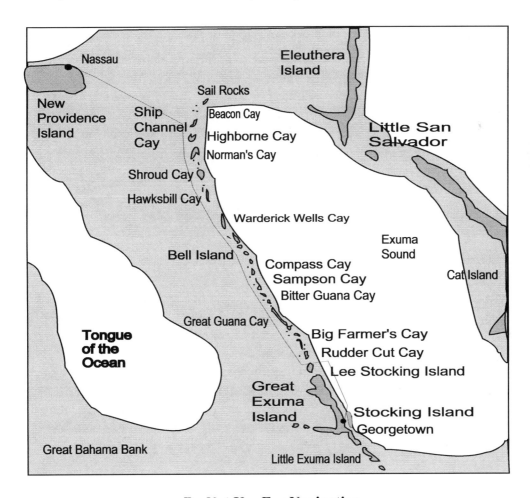

Follow the instructions found in the cruising guide referenced above for guidance in cruising down the Exuma chain. Appendix C shows how I have rated the harbors from Nassau to Georgetown and you should notice how limited really good anchorages are. The drawing on the previous page will assist you in visualizing where the many different islands I refer to are located. I will cover most of the major islands as you proceed south. It is certainly not necessary to stop at every island along the way, but most cruisers do stop at a number of them. For those in a hurry, the 120 nautical mile trip can be made in two to three days with good weather.

The route from Nassau to Georgetown requires careful navigation. For the most part, a vessel can travel SE from Nassau to the west side of the Exuma Islands and work their way south on the protected Great Bahama Bank until reaching Lee Stocking Island. At that point most vessels pass through a cut to the Exuma Sound and make their way to Georgetown via deep water.

The waters around the Exuma Islands are filled with reefs and shallow spots. Strong storms continue to move shoals all the time. Being able to "read" the water is essential for a carefree passage south to Georgetown. Be sure to follow the navigation waypoints on the recommended charts and cruising guide.

Departing Nassau

You will not have any place to stop except open water for the first 30 nautical miles after you leave Nassau. For many vessels, this means planning on spending the night at one of the first Exuma Islands you encounter.

Following the appropriate charts, work your way east out of Nassau to Porgee Rock. From Porgee Rock a vessel can head directly to any of three points near Highborne Cay. In route your vessel will pass over the Yellow Bank. There are numerous uncharted coral heads in the water of the Yellow Bank. Be sure to keep a sharp lookout for these dark ominous structures under water and pass to one side or the other of them. In theory, you can carry 5'MLW over all the coral heads, however, I wouldn't push my luck.

You want to schedule your trip so that you pass over the Yellow Bank close to high noon. This will give you the best visibility in the water.

Ship Channel Cay

There is a fair harbor south of Ship Channel Cay between Roberts Cay and Long Rock. The 4'MLW entrance channel leads to 7'MLW anchorage in a class C harbor. All of the islands in the vicinity of this harbor are uninhabited. Ship Channel Cay has remains from when it was involved in the lumber industry.

On the western side of Ship Channel Cay there is a fair weather class F harbor if you are not up to finding your way into the better anchorage.

There is excellent fishing and underwater exploring in and around Ship Channel Cay. However, the eastern side is strewn with reefs and great care should be taken while exploring this area.

Allens Cay

The several islands in the vicinity of Allens Cay are uninhabited except by Iguanas. This is the primary reason most first time visitors stop here. The recommended anchorage is between Allens and Leaf Cay. The anchorage is only a class E harbor, and several high-speed passenger excursion vessels from Nassau make daily calls. But, the Iguanas make it a worthwhile stop in good weather.

The Iguanas are located on both SW Allens and Leaf Cay. They are protected and you must not harm them. Visitors are asked not to feed the iguanas, however, it seems everyone does and the iguanas have now come to expect it. Do not take pets ashore on either SW Allens or Leaf Cay.

Highbourne Cay

This was the first inhabited island in the northern Exumas and today it is private with a restricted community. There is a marina, Highbourne Cay Marina, large grocery, gift shop and liquor store. The fairly protected class B harbor is on the south side of the island on the west side. The marina provides transient docking, a dinghy dock, fuel, water, laundry, resaurant and trash disposal. There are no longer any mooring balls in the cay. The best anchorage in in 10 to 15 feet of water to the west of the cay. A second, smaller anchorage is within the cut on the eastern side. Holding here is just fair. The charted anchorage in the northern cove is subject to any surge from swells in the sound.

Normans Cay

Normans Cay is one of the largest islands in the Exuma chain and is best known for its history of drug smuggling. Today the shot up remains of a building, abandoned buildings and a crashed airplane, residue of this history, can be seen near the southern anchorage. The island is inhabited, and the former McDuff's has reopened under a new name, the Norman's Cay Beach Club. Adjacent to the club is a small airstrip.

The anchorage at the southern end is the more popular of the two, because it is easiest to get in to. However this class E harbor is very uncomfortable in an east wind.

The better of the two anchorages is in the center of the island and virtually surrounded on all sides. This class A harbor is only accessible from the Exuma Sound side and will carry 6'MLW. Because of the entrance from deep water and the lack of channel markers, this harbor should only be entered or exited during good weather.

Atlantis is an upscale resort and marina in Nassau that reminds you a lot of Las Vegas. Expect the same high prices!

There are a number of caves to explore as well as abandoned structures on the island. Note: The property north of the new club is private property and you should refrain from trespassing.

As with all Exuma Islands some vessels choose to simply anchor on the west side of the island in the lee from eastern winds in what would be classified as a class F harbor.

The Exuma Cays Land and Sea Park

This park, often referred to as the Warderick Wells Park because the headquarters is there, extends over a 22-mile area starting just south of Normans Cay at Wax Cay and running south to Compass Cay. Established in 1958 it is one of 26 National Parks and Protected Areas managed by the Bahamas National Trust. The website address is www.exumapark.info.

The park is a No Take Zone and marine protected area and thus has some special rules that are strictly enforced. A violation will result in severe penalties. Briefly, these rules state that you cannot fish, hunt or pick any vegetation. You are not permitted to deface the park either on land or underwater. If you take a pet ashore it must be on a leash. Do not leave any trash behind. Anchoring is permitted only in the Hog Cay anchorage to the south. Do not anchor such that your anchor or chain will damage coral or underwater structures. You may not remain within the park more than 14 consecutive days. You are encouraged to read the complete list of rules on the website.

There are 11 cays in the park. Three are described in this chapter. Complete details of the mooring fields discussed may be found on the park website.

Shroud Cay
(Located in the park)

Flat and wide, the shallow water, coral heads and sand bars extend nearly a mile to the west of Shroud Cay. There are several anchorages along the west side of the island but they offer little better than a class F harbor.

Shroud Cay is uninhabited and offers a very interesting and scenic place to visit. The many shallow creeks offer ample place to explore by dinghy. The shallow water gets quite warm in the sun and makes it a great place to swim. Do not be tempted by the fish, conch or lobsters you may see, remember this is part of the park.

On the island itself is a fresh water well frequently used by cruisers to restock water supplies. The water is very good. There is also an area called Camp Driftwood that was built by a hermit and can best be described as Robinson Crusoe's island home.

There is a mooring field 1.5 miles NE of the northern tip of Elbow Cay. They are available on a first come, first served basis. A payment box is located at the north end of the beach at the north end of the mooring field.

All in all, Shroud Cay offers the best the Exumas has to offer in terms of life ashore with great beaches, isolation, unique things to see and wildlife.

Hawksbill Cay
(Located in the park)

Easily one of the prettiest islands in the Exuma chain, Hawksbill Cay is uninhabited and has beaches on both sides. There are ruins to explore, a fresh water well, and a large cave. The cay has two mooring fields with 4 moorings in the north field and 10 moorings in the south field. The north field is on the westside one-half way down the cay. The south field is on the southern tip of the cay. Both are first come, first served and the payment box is in the southern field adjacent to the Exuma Cays Land & Sea Park sign. The cut at the south end of the island has a particularly strong tidal current and should be explored with caution.

Warderick Wells Cay

Warderick Wells Cay is home to the park rangers and provides three mooring fields. North of the Visitor Center in the "J" shaped harbor you will find 22 mooring balls. Just south of the Visitor Center you will find 26 mooring locations. The south harbor with 6 moorings is on the eastern side of the island and only offers a class E harbor.

Whenever approaching Warderick Wells, call the park rangers by hailing Exuma Park on VHF 09 during business hours, (9am to 12 pm, 1 pm to 4 pm M-Sa, 9 am to noon Su) and request mooring assignment. The fee for vessels under 40 feet is $15/night. For 40-50 feet it is $20/night. Fees are higher for larger vessels.

Ashore there is a brackish well, some ruins to visit and the usual flora and fauna. Warderick Wells is reputed to be haunted. A skeleton was found on the beach several years ago and in the ensuing confusion, the skull ended up in Georgetown and the remainder of the skeleton was buried on Warderick Wells. So if you see a headless skeleton wandering around at night, do not be alarmed, he is only looking for his head….or yours.

Bell Island

Bell Island offers two anchorages but not much else. This privately owned island is being renovated and visitors are discouraged. The eastern anchorage in Harbour Bay is class E, while the western side of the island is class F.

Compass Cay

North of Compass Cay is Conch Cut and the southern border of the Warderick Wells Park. South of this point you may again fish and take shellfish. Compass Cay offers a large salty pond in the middle and a small marina, Compass Cay Marina, in the protected center. The entrance from the banks was dredged in 2007 and is reported to be 7' deep. Confirm this prior to entering. The anchorage on the south side of Compass Cay between Compass Cay and Pipe Cay is a class D harbor. Further inside Compass Cay is the more protected Compass Cay Marina and a small mooring ball area providing a class B harbor. Only five or six vessels can use this harbor at a time. Mooring balls are available for a fee.

There is a deep-water entrance to the class B harbor on Compass Cay from the Exuma Sound side entering just south of Compass Cay.

Compass Cay and the adjacent cays are all privately owned and do not afford the cruiser a place to roam.

Sampson Cay

Sampson Cay has no community, but does sport one of the better marinas, Sampson Cay Marina, along this stretch of the Exumas. The marina is located on the western side of the island well protected by a peninsula providing a class A harbor with room for about 30 boats. The marina offers fuel, electricity, dockage, small store and a restaurant. There is no anchoring and no mooring balls in the marina basin. The facilities completed an extensive upgrade a few years ago and offers diesel and gas as well as a small chandlery.

Sampson Cay also offers seaplane service for those that need to be elsewhere and return to their vessel at a later date. This is one of the few secure marinas where you could leave your vessel for a prolonged period in the Exumas. Just outside the marina is a class C harbor with an anchorage. The mooring balls previously installed here are gone.

Staniel Cay

This island is located between Sampson and Bitter Guana Cays. This very popular island has a small community, a marina, Staniel Cay Yacht Club, and offers easy access to Thunderball Cave where the James Bond movie, of the same name, was filmed. Note, the docks at the yacht club are untenable in north or west winds.

The community on Staniel Cay boasts three stores, two restaurants, an airfield, and several bars. The anchorage and marinas are located on the northwest shore in a class D harbor. Mooring balls, for a small fee, have been placed in the vicinity of Thunderball Cave.

Besides the lively community on Staniel Cay you can swim and snorkel in the clear water in the area. There are beaches and paths all over the island. A must visit to Thunderball Cave should be made by dinghy at or near slack tide. The current flows through that area at a good clip.

A better anchorage for Staniel Cay is located just north and to the west of Big Major Spot and provides a class B harbor. The downside is that it becomes a 1½-mile dinghy ride to Staniel Cay. However, the more comfortable anchorage may be worth it.

Bitter Guana Cay

Bitter Guana Cay has little to offer the visiting cruiser. It is best known for the mass grave of Haitians on the island. They were killed in a shipwreck just east of the cay. Just to the south of Bitter Guana Cay is Dotham Cut, one of the more popular inlets to the Exuma Sound.

Great Guana Cay

The longest island in the Exuma chain, Great Guana Cay provides the best class F

harbor in the prevailing easterly winds. The 12-mile long island provides several good anchorages along the western shore and has the largest community, Black Point, in the Exuma Chain, except for Georgetown.

Black Point has a small store, clinic, phone company office, restaurant and airfield. There are some pretty beaches on the west shore with several small-protected bays. Watch for a number of coral heads as you explore this shoreline. Once ashore you can walk to the ocean side, explore some of the many caves or ruins or just enjoy beach combing.

If you tuck in real close in Little Bay, you could almost upgrade this to a class C harbor. However, when a front comes through, the SW winds would make it very uncomfortable.

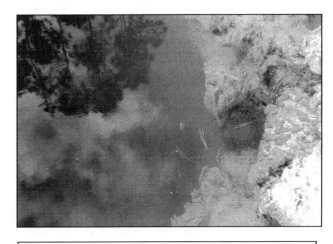

Looking down into a "blue hole". The water can be hundreds of feet deep. The incoming and outgoing tide creates strong currents at the entrance.

Great Guana Cay was scheduled to become the home of the Great Guana Marina & Resort. Construction has reportedly stopped.

Little Farmer's Cay

Little Farmer's Cay is located just west of Big Farmer's Cay. While Big Farmer's Cay is largely uninhabited and has little to offer, Little Farmer's Cay has a picturesque village and marina, Farmer's Cay Yacht Club. The very small marina is located on the NE corner of Little Farmer's Cay in a class D harbor and offers fuel, dockage and moorings at a fee.

In the small community further south in Little Harbour you can anchor in a class E harbor and you will find a clinic, grocery, liquor store, post office and restaurants. The neatly laid out and colorful community is sure to inspire you as the perfect Bahamian village.

Rudder Cut Cay

Rudder Cut Cay was best known for having the only class A harbor where vessels could anchor, go ashore, fill up their water tanks for free from abandoned cisterns and generally relax and wait for bad weather to pass. The entrance channel would carry 5'MLW and was used by hundreds of cruisers in the past. Today it is closed to boaters and visitors are not welcome ashore or in the harbor.

Just to the south of Rudder Cut Cay is Little Darby Island and the class B harbor there does offer good protection in what used to be a German U-Boat harbor. This harbor also carries 5'MLW at the entrance channel and vessels can anchor in 10-15' in very good protection. This is also a private island.

Lee Stocking Island

You should plan on anchoring in the protection of either Little Darby Island above, or Lee Stocking Island while waiting for good weather to cross the Exuma Sound to Georgetown. There are two class C harbors on the west shore of Lee Stocking Island. Lee Stocking Island is privately owned and home to the Caribbean Marine Research Center (CRMC). Before going ashore contact CRMC on VHF 16 by the call name of Bahama Hunter. You usually can arrange a tour of this interesting research facility and get permission to wander ashore.

To the NW is Norman's Pond Cay. This unique cay is a 1 to 2 mile dinghy ride and well worth the visit. Entrance to the large salt pond can be made on the western shore at high tide via the old canal. Inside you can see the remains of what was once a salt farming adventure. There are iguanas on the island and pets are not permitted. On the NW shore of Norman's Pond Cay is one of the best examples of underwater caves in the Bahamas. A must for divers with scuba gear. It should not be explored by snorkel equipment only.

On To Georgetown

Most cruisers will wait in the protection of Little Darby Cay or Lee Stocking Island and wait for a good day to cross the Exuma Sound. It is a 25-mile journey over very deep water with entrance to a narrow channel that can be very dangerous in rough seas. You should not depart the protection of the Great Bahama Bank for Georgetown unless weather conditions are correct and the weather forecast is for good weather all day.

A new marina opened in 2006 on Great Exuma Island. Located just 10 miles north of Georgetown, access is made directly from Exuma Sound. The Marina at Emerald Bay is part of Emerald Bay Resort located just north of

Junkanoo is celebrated throughout the Bahamas on Boxing Day, the day after Christmas, and includes colorfully dressed dancers in a noisy parade with parties and fun for all.

Ocean Bight. The entrance channel can be found at N23° 38.23 and W75° 54.44. Don't try this channel without first contacting the marina, and don't try it in bad weather. The channel passes just north of Poor Betty Cay and the new basin is clearly shown on chart EX23 of the recommended chart kit. This class A marina gives you a place to stop and hole up in the worst weather. More importantly you can leave your vessel there, ride the 10 miles south to Georgetown and take an airplane to wherever you need to be. Like some other new developments in the Bahamas, it is reportedly struggling in the current economic conditions.

Entrance to the Elizabeth Harbour at Georgetown is made through Conch Cay Cut and the approach and navigation points are given in the cruising guide and charts recommended in this chapter. Entering the harbor requires several turns to avoid reefs and this trip should not be made without (1) a GPS and the charts and guides above or in lieu of this by (2) following someone in who has local knowledge or the required GPS and charts.

Georgetown

Mecca, the pot of gold at the end of the rainbow, the end of most cruisers winter journey. The trip from the states has been long and interesting. Most cruisers in winter will spend the next two to three months at anchor in Georgetown enjoying what the area has to offer. There are no places nearby where you can go for a day trip like there are in the Abacos and once here, you are here for the duration.

Georgetown offers just about everything a cruiser could want in the way of goods and services. There are groceries, restaurants, banks, stores, churches, hardware, tourist shops, liquor store, phone office and airfield. Exuma Docking Services (hail "Sugar One") is open for transients however it is exposed to southwest winds and may be prone to surge in easterly winds. Kidd Cove Marina is on the peninsula opposite the government docks. It is the base for Bahamas Houseboats rental fleet but may have transient space. The class C harbor can be very rough in eastern winds.

Entrance to the town from the anchorage is made under a bridge into Lake Victoria where a large dinghy dock has been provided for the visiting cruisers that will often number near 500.

Outside the town, most activities take place on Stocking Island located just east of Georgetown. There is usually a take away at Hamburger Beach and a small restaurant operated near Hole #0. Stocking Island offers three class A harbors, holes #0, #2, and #3. Unfortunately, with only room for 6-8 boats in each, they quickly fill up with the first few of the 500 or so boats that show up each winter. Entrance to Holes #2 and #3 can handle a 6' draft vessel at MLW. However Hole #0 is shoal draft and often referred to as the Multihull hole. Mooring balls pretty well tie up hole #0. Arrangements can be made to leave your vessel in Hole #0 on a mooring ball for a period. Hole #1 offers a class B harbor but fills up quickly. Southeast about two miles there are three more class B harbors in the area of Crab Cay and Red Shank Cays. They too fill up quickly. In reality, most cruisers end up anchored in Elizabeth Harbour between Georgetown and Stocking Island. With prevailing east winds most vessels anchor close to Stocking Island. When a cold front comes through with its associated strong NW winds, the class C Elizabeth Harbour can be a rough place to lay at anchor.

The cruisers are very organized. Some complain too organized. The Cruisers Net starts off each day announcing the day's activities and it usually includes volleyball on Volleyball Beach or a cook out on Hamburger Beach. The big event each year is the Cruising Regatta that usually takes place near the end of March. It includes races, games, contests and fun for all. Most cruisers thoroughly enjoy themselves while in Georgetown spending days walking on the beaches, swimming on the sound side of Stocking Island, and just cavorting with fellow cruisers.

Remember the warning about swimming in Elizabeth Harbour. With 500 boats dumping their black waste directly overboard, you should not swim in these waters. Reserve your swimming for the more open sound side of stocking island.

Georgetown does offer an airport and many cruisers have friends and relatives join them here by air. Exumas Docking Service is one place you can leave your boat for a period. A better choice would be to go back up the Exuma chain and leave your vessel at Sampson Cay Marina.

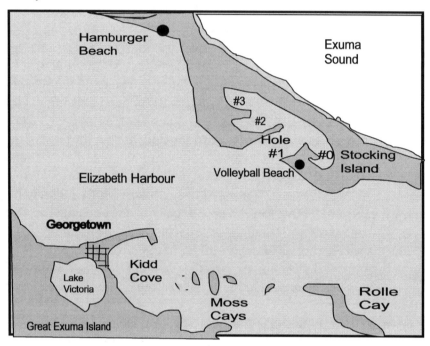

Summary

Returning to the states from Georgetown is easy, following the directions that brought you here in reverse. If you should choose to explore Long Island, Eleuthera, or some more distant place in the Bahamas you should have the following guides and charts on board.

- **Waterway Guide Bahamas 2013 Edition**
- **NV-Charts Chartbook Region 9.3**
- **Explorer Chartbook Far Bahamas**

While Andros and Eleuthera are remote, they do offer interesting and exciting cruising for those that feel the desire to explore these more pristine locations. There is a good possibility that you will have made close friends with some more experienced cruisers while staying in Georgetown and it would be wise to travel with a buddy boat to these locations for your first visit.

The primary purpose of this book was to assist you in deciding if you could go to the Bahamas, assist you in planning your first trip if you did choose to go, and finally, give you an idea of what you might find once you got there. It was not intended to replace any of the recommended cruising guides or chart kits.

Appendix A

Recommended Charts and Cruising Guides

(Pricing as of November 2012)

The recommended publications are listed by area. Note that there is some duplication between areas. You obviously only need one copy of any recommended chart kit or cruising guide and you need not purchase the ones for areas you do not intend to visit.

The northern Bahamas (Abacos)

- **Waterway Guide, Bahamas 2013 Edition*,** $39.95
- **NV-Charts Chartbook Region 9.1,** $79.95
- **Explorer Chartbook Near Bahamas,** by Monty U Sara Lewis $59.95
- **The Cruising Guide to Abaco Bahamas,** by Steve Dodge $24.95
- **Great Abaco and Cays Chart, AB001,** (Optional) $19.95

The southern Bahamas (Exumas)

- **Waterway Guide, Bahamas 2013 Edition*,** $39.95
- **NV-Charts Chartbook Region 9.2,** $79.95
- **Explorer Chartbook Exumas,** By Monty and Sara Lewis $59.95
- **Explorer Chartbook Near Bahamas,** by Monty & Sara Lewis $59.95
- **The Exuma Guide,** by Stephen Pavlidis $39.95

Distance Places (Eleuthera, Long Island, Andros)

- **Waterway Guide, Bahamas 2013 Edition*,** $39.95
- **NV-Charts Chartbook Region 9.3,** $79.95
- **Explorer Chartbook Far Bahamas,** $59.95

* Also includes The Turks and Caicos Islands

NV-Charts set of three $149.95

Appendix B

Crossing the Gulf Stream

One of the problems the mariner encounters when crossing the Gulf Stream is how to allow for the set of the current. Fast boats have little trouble correcting the effect of the Gulf Stream, but boats with operating speeds of between 5 and 10 knots must make major corrections. Here are some corrected courses and estimated elapsed times at varying speeds under normal sea conditions.

This table should be used only as a guide, not as a reference. Varying wind and weather conditions will influence your passage.

This table should give a general idea of how long your crossing might take under normal conditions. The chart below depicts those rhumb line crossings noted in the tables and can be used in conjunction with your LORAN or GPS headings.

- The Gulf Stream was arbitrarily figured at 001 degrees true, 2.5 knots for runs to Lake Worth Inlet and at 002 degrees true, 2.6 knots, for all other runs.
- Variation used was 004.5 degrees west.
- Crossings to Lucaya extend beyond the Gulf Stream's effect. Thus, the rhumb line distance shown is that used in calculations for the current, followed by the rhumb line distance to complete the run without current to offset.
- Some routes to Lucaya could not be a single, direct run. They were computed to a point off Southwest Point on Grand Bahama Island, then to the buoy off Bell Channel.
- All runs are not the reverse of others. Miami to West End is calculated, but not West End to Miami because the Gulf Stream would be too much "on the nose." Lake Worth Inlet to Bimini is not calculated for the same reason.

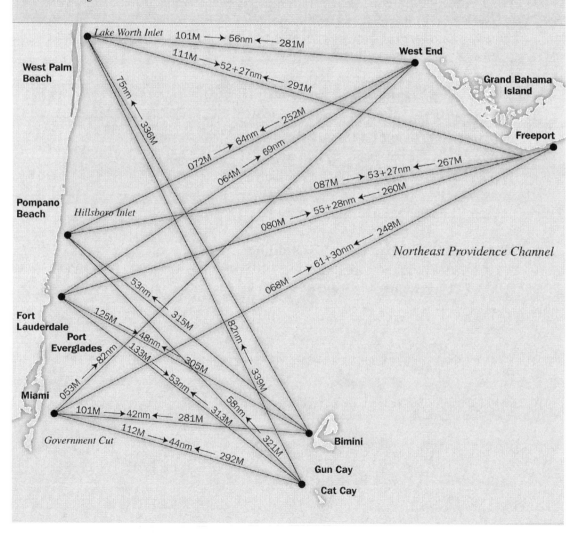

Chart from Waterway Guide Bahamas 2013 edition.

Eastbound to the Bahamas

RLC / RLD	From / To	5 CS/EET	6 CS/EET	8 CS/EET	10 CS/EET	12 CS/EET	15 CS/EET	20 CS/EET
101	Lake Worth Inlet	131	126	119	115	113	111	108
56	West End	13/20	10/31	7/30	5/52	4/49	3/49	2/50
111	Lake Worth Inlet	140	135	129	125	123	120	118
52	Lucaya	19/04	15/04	10/45	8/23	6/54	5/27	4/02
+27	(via SW Point)							
72	Hillsboro Inlet	100	95	89	85	83	81	79
64	West End	11/24	9/32	7/15	5/52	4/56	4/00	3/02
87	Hillsboro Inlet	118	112	106	102	99	97	94
53	Lucaya	16/20	13/22	9/54	7/53	6/34	5/16	3/57
+27	(via SW Point)							
64	Port Everglades	89	85	79	76	74	72	70
69	West End	11/28	9/43	7/30	6/08	5/11	4/13	3/14
80	Port Everglades	109	104	98	94	92	89	87
55	Lucaya	16/10	13/22	10/00	8/01	6/42	5/23	4/03
+28								
125	Port Everglades	154	148	142	139	136	134	132
48	Bimini	14/38	10/57	7/22	5/36	4/31	3/31	2/34
133	Port Everglades	159	154	149	145	143	141	139
53	Gun Cay	17/20	12/47	8/29	6/23	5/07	3/57	2/53
53	Miami	74	71	66	63	62	60	58
82	West End	12/33	10/48	8/29	7/00	5/58	4/54	3/46
68	Miami	94	90	84	81	79	77	74
61	Lucaya	16/29	13/50	10/31	8/30	7/09	5/46	4/23
+30								
101	Miami	132	127	120	116	114	111	108
42	Bimini	10/03	8/28	5/37	4/23	3/37	2/52	2/08
112	Miami	142	137	130	127	124	122	119
44	Gun Cay	11/49	9/04	6/17	4/50	3/57	3/06	2/17

Westbound to Florida

RLC / RLD	From / To	5 CS/EET	6 CS/EET	8 CS/EET	10 CS/EET	12 CS/EET	15 CS/EET	20 CS/EET
281	West End	251	256	263	267	269	271	274
56	Lake Worth Inlet	12/33	10/01	7/15	5/42	4/43	3/45	2/48
252	West End	224	229	235	239	241	243	245
64	Hillsboro Inlet	19/41	14/42	9/53	7/29	6/02	4/42	3/26
291	Lucaya	262	267	273	277	279	282	284
52	Lake Worth Inlet	15/57	13/06	9/44	7/46	6/28	5/11	3/54
+27	(via SW Point)							
267	Lucaya	236	242	248	252	255	257	260
53	Hillsboro Inlet	19/29	15/20	10/54	8/30	6/59	5/31	4/06
+27	(via SW Point)							
260	Lucaya	231	236	242	246	248	251	253
55	Port Everglades	21/17	16/33	11/38	9/01	7/23	5/09	4/18
+28								
248	Lucaya	222	226	232	235	237	239	242
61	Miami	25/27	19/25	13/10	10/15	8/20	6/31	4/47
+30								
336	Bimini	320	322	326	328	329	331	332
75	Lake Worth Inlet	10/45	9/22	7/28	6/13	5/19	4/23	3/23
315	Bimini	290	294	300	303	305	307	309
53	Hillsboro Inlet	8/44	7/25	5/44	4/41	3/58	3/14	2/28
305	Bimini	277	282	288	291	294	296	298
48	Port Everglades	8/38	7/12	5/28	4/25	3/43	3/00	2/17
281	Bimini	250	255	262	266	268	271	273
42	Miami	9/38	7/38	6/16	4/55	4/04	3/14	2/25
339	Gun Cay	324	326	330	332	333	334	335
82	Lake Worth Inlet	11/35	10/07	8/05	6/44	5/47	4/46	3/42
321	Gun Cay	298	302	307	310	312	314	315
58	Hillsboro Inlet	9/08	7/49	6/06	5/01	4/16	3/29	2/41
313	Gun Cay	287	292	297	301	302	305	307
53	Port Everglades	8/53	7/31	5/47	4/43	4/00	3/15	2/29
292	Gun Cay	262	267	274	277	280	282	285
44	Miami	8/59	7/18	5/23	4/17	3/34	2/52	2/09

KEY. RLC: Rhumb line Course (degrees magnetic); RLD: Rhumb line Distance (nautical miles); CS: Course Steered (degrees magnetic); EET: Estimated Elapsed Time (hours/minutes)

EXAMPLE. The Rhumb line Course from Lake Worth Inlet to West End is 099 degrees magnetic, over the Rhumb line distance of 56 nautical miles. At 5 knots, you would steer a magnetic course of 129 degrees to offset the effects of the Gulf Stream. The passage would take roughly 13 hours and 20 minutes.

Chart from Waterway Guide Bahamas 2012 edition.

Bahamas Bound

Appendix C - Cruising Stores For 3 Months

Item	3 Mo	Item	3 Mo
Apple Sauce	2	Ketchup	1
Apricots	2	Kleenex	1
Beans, Baked	3	Kool Aid	5
Beans, Black, Can	4	Macaroni	6
Beans, Green	8	Macaroni, w/cheese	3
Beans, Kidney	6	Marshmallow, Whip,	1
Beans, Pinto	3	Meat, Bacon	2
Beets	2	Meat, Beef	8
Bisquick	2	Meat, Chicken	16
Bleach, 1 gallon	2	Meat, Pork	8
Bug Spray	2	Meat, Turkey, Ground	16
Butter, 1 LB	2	Meat, Turkey Thigh	2
Bread Crumbs	1	Milk, Box, Skim	10
Cake Mix	2	Milk, Evaporated	3
Carrots	8	Milk, Powered, Pk	10
Cereal, Oat	1	Miracle Whip	3
Cereal, Box	7	Mushrooms	8
Cheese, Parmensan	2	Napkins, Pack	1
Cheese, Velvita	1	Noodles, Egg	2
Chips, Tortilla	4	Noodles, Lasagna	1
Chili	2	Noodles, Spaghetti, 1 #	8
Chocolate Chip, 1 LB	1	Oil, 32 oz	1
Cocoa, Can	1	Olives, Black	1
Coffee, Decaf	1	Olives, Green	2
Coffee, Regular	1	Pancake Mix	2
Cookies	3	Paper Plates, Pack	1
Corn, Whole Kernel	8	Paper Towels	6
Crackers, Graham	3	Peaches	6
Crackers, Oyster	2	Pears	3
Crackers, Snack	6	Peas	4
Crackers, Soda	2	Peanut Butter	2
Cranberry Sauce	1	Pie Filling	2
Crystal Lite, Tube	8	Pickles, Sweet	2
Deodorant	2	Pineapple	2
Dream Whip	3	Pop Corn, Microwave,	6
Eggs, Dozen	2	Potato, Mashed, Inst	2
Flour, White, 5#	2	Potato, Sweet, Can	3
Flour, Whole Wheat, #5	2	Potato, White, Can	4
Fruit, Mixed, can	6	Raisins, 1 LB Box	1
Frosting	2	Razors	6
Gravy, Package	6	Relish	1
Jelly	2	Rice, 5 LB	2
Juice, Cranberry,	6	Salmon	6

Item	3 Mo
Salsa	2
Salt	1
Sauce, Spaghetti	12
Sauerkraut	4
Season All	1
Shampoo, Head &	1
Shampoo, Suave	1
Shaving Cream	1
Shortening, Crisco	1
Soap, Hand	6
Soap, Dish	2
Soap, Laundry	2
Soap, Soft Scrub	1
Soap, Spic and Span	1
Soup, Broth	4
Soup, Chunky	3
Soup, Mushroom	5
Soup, Tomato	3
Soup, Ramen	7
Spam	6
Spinach	2
Sugar, Brown 1#	1
Sugar, White 5#	1
Sweet and Low, box	1
Syrup, Pancake	2
Toilet Tissue	6
Toothpaste	1
Tomato, Stewed	7
Trash Bags, box	1
Tuna, Can	12
Vanilla	1
Vinegar, Gal	2
Yeast, jar	1
Zip Lock Freezer Bag	1
Zip Lock Sandwich Bag	3
Zip Lock Storage Bag	2

Bahamas Harbor Rating Guide

Harbors in the Bahamas offer different degrees of protection. Some are excellent. Others are terrible and should be considered fair weather anchorages only. The chart below defines the different class of harbors and anchorages as I see them in the Bahamas. Harbors may provide an anchorage, mooring balls, marina or any combination of the three. I will rate each harbor and tell you whether it contains room for anchoring, has mooring balls or marina(s).

Class A – This harbor has a very narrow entrance, very little tidal current flow, and is well protected from all wind directions. This harbor is calm in almost every wind condition.

Class B – This harbor is open to one direction (<60 degrees), but not the ocean. It provides protection in all wind directions except one. There is little tidal current flow. This harbor is uncomfortable in the strong winds from the wrong direction.

Class C – This harbor is open in two or more directions (<120 degrees), but not the ocean side. There is little current flow. This harbor is uncomfortable in strong winds from several directions.

Class D – This harbor is open in two or more directions (<120 degrees), but not the ocean side. There is substantial tidal current flow. This harbor is very uncomfortable in strong winds opposing currents within the harbor.

Class E – This harbor is open in two or more directions (<120 degrees), and one side leads to the open ocean. There is substantial current flow. This harbor is very uncomfortable in strong winds from one direction and may be untenable in strong winds from the ocean side.

Class F – This harbor is protected only on one side. It is exposed more than 240 degrees. There is little tidal current. This harbor is only comfortable in winds from one quadrant. In shifting winds this harbor is very uncomfortable.

Class G – This harbor is open in all directions (such as anchoring on the banks), but provides protection from very large waves by virtue of its shallow depth. This would be a very uncomfortable anchorage in any strong wind.

Appendix E – Marina Transient Rates

Rates in effect November 2012

Name	Season 1	Tran $/ft	Elect	Water	Season 2	Tran $/ft	Elect	Water
Abaco Beach Resort	Sept 8 to Feb 28	$2.75/ft	$0.65/KWh	$0.15/gal	Mar 1 to Sept 7	$3.25/ft	$0.65/KWh	$0.15/gal
Baker's Bay Club	All Year	$3.00/ft			Mooring $25/day			
Berry Islands Club	All Year	$1.00/ft	$0.47/KWh	$0.35/gal				
Bimini Bay Resort and Marina	Sept 15 to Mar 24	$2.00/ft	$0.60/KWh	$0.45/gal	Apr 16 to Sept 14	$3.00/ft	$0.60/KWh	$0.45/gal
Bimini Big Game Marina	Oct 1 to mar 31	$1.50/ft	$15/day+	$0.30/gal	Apr 1 to Sep 30	$2.50/ft	$15/day+	$0.30/gal
Bimini Blue Water Resort	All Year	$1.00/ft	$10/day+	$0.60/gal				
Bimini Sands Resort & Marina	All Year	$1.10/ft	$10/day	$0.20/gal				
Black Sound Marina	All Year	$1.00/ft	$15/day+	$0.30/gal				
Bluff House Club and Marina	Sep 1 to Mar 31	$0.90/ft	$12.50+/dy	$0.20/gal	Apr 1 to Aug 31	$2.00/ft	$12.50+/dy	$0.20/gal
Boat Harbour Marina	Sep 9 to Feb 28	$2.75/ft	$0.65/KWh	$0.15/gal	Mar 1 to Sept 8	$3.25/ft	$0.65/KWh	$0.15/gal
Browns Hotel & Marina	All Year	$1.75/ft	$20/day +	$0.30/gal				
Cat Cay Yacht Club	All Year	$3.25/ft	$0.65/KWh	$0.40/gal				
Chub Cay Marina	Jul 25 to Feb 17	$2.75/ft	$0.65/KWh	$0.40/gal	Feb 18 to Jul 24	$4.35/ft	$0.65/KWh	$0.40/gal
Compass Cay Marina	All Year	$2.50/ft	$40/day+	$0.50/gal				
Conch Inn Marina	Sep 1 to Feb 28	$1.20/ft	$0.55/KWh	$12 min	Mar 1 to Aug 31	$1.40/ft	$0.55/KWh	$12 min
Emerald Bay Marina	All Year	$2.25/ft	$0.85/KWh	$0.40/gal				
Exuma Docking Services	All Year	$1.00/ft	$10/day+	$0.20/gal				
Farmers Cay Yacht Club	All Year	$1.50/ft	$15/day+	$0.50/gal	Moorings $10/day			
Grand Bahama Yacht Club	Oct 1 to Feb 28	$1.40/ft	$0.45/KWh	$5/day	Mar 1 to Sept 30	$1.70/ft	$0.45/KWh	$5/day
	weekly	$1.20/ft			weekly	$1.60/ft		
Great Harbour Cay Marina	All Year	$1.50/ft	$0.75/KWh	$0.50/gal				
Green Turtle Club Marina	See website							
Harbour View Marina	Sep 1 to Feb 28	$1.50/ft	$18/day +	$0.20/gal	Mar 1 to Aug 31	$1.90/ft	$18/day +	$0.20/gal
Highborne Cay Marina	All Year	$2.10/ft+	$25/day+	$0.50/gal				
Hope Town Inn & Marina	All Year	$1.00/ft	$0.65/KWh	$0.25/gal	16 moorings also available @ $20/day.			
Hurricane Hole Marina	All Year	$4.00/ft	$0.65/KWh	$0.25/gal				

Bahamas Bound
Appendix E – Marina Transient Rates

Name	Season 1	Tran $/ft	Elect	Water	Season 2	Tran $/ft	Elect	Water
Lighthouse Marina	All Year	$1.00/ft	$10/day+	$0.25/gal	Boat yard.			
Man-O-War Marina	All Year	$1.60/ft	$15/day+	$0.20/gal	Moorings also available @ $17/day			
Mangoes	Sep 1 to April 1	$1.20/ft	$0.60/KWh	$5/day	Apr 1 to Sep 1	$1.50/ft	$0.60KWh	$5/day
Marina at Atlantis	Nov 16 to Aug 15	$4.00/ft +	$0.65/KWh	$0.25/gal	Aug 16 to Nov 13	$3.00/ft +	$0.65/KWh	$0.25/gal
Marsh Harbour Marina	All Year	$1.40/ft	$0.60/KWh	$4/day				
Nassau Yacht Haven	All Year	$2.00/ft	$0.65/KWh	$10/day				
Nassau Harbour Club	Call for current rates.							
Ocean Reef Yacht Club	All Year	$1.25/ft	$0.50/KWh	Included				
Old Bahama Bay Marina	Sep 7 to Mar 31	$2.00/ft	$0.70/ft+	$15/day+	Apr 1 to Sep 6	$3.05/ft	$0.70/ft+	$15/day+
Orchid Bay Marina	All Year	$1.95/ft	$0.60/KWh	$0.30/gal				
Other Shore Club, The	All Year	$0.80/ft	$12/day+	$0.30/gal				
Port Lucaya Marina	Low season	$1.85/ft	$0.45/KWh	$10/day	High Season	$2.20/ft+	$0.45/KWh	$10/day
Rosie's Place	All Year	$0.75/ft	$10/day+	$0.25/gal				
Sampson Cay Marina	All Year	$2.75/ft	Metered	$0.50/gal				
Sea Crest Marina	All Year	$1.00/ft	$14/day+	$0.30/gal				
Sea Spray Marina	Sept 1 to Feb 28	$1.90/ft	$0.65/KWh	$0.40/gal	Jan 1 to Aug 31	$1.90/ft	$0.65/KWh	$0.40/gal
Spanish Cay Marina	Sep 15 to Mar 14	$1.50/ft	$20/day+	$0.25/gal	Mar 15 to Sep 14	$2.75/ft	$20/day+	$0.25/gal
Staniel Cay Yacht Club	All Year	$2.00/ft	$0.75/KWh	$0.40/gal				
Treasure Cay Marina	Sept 1 to Mar 31	$1.30/ft	$17/day+	$7/day	Apr 1 to Aug 31	$1.95/ft	$17/day+	$7/day
Walkers Cay Marina	Call for rates.							
Weech's Bimini Dock	All Year	$0.85/ft	$15/day+	NA				
Xanadu Beach Marina	Sep 1 to Mar 31	$1.05/ft	$20/day	$10/day	Apr 1 to Aug 31	$1.20/ft	$20/day	$10/day

Appendix F – Monthly Marina Rates

Rates in effect November 2012

Name	Season 1	Month $/ft	Elect	Water	Season 2	Month $/ft	Elect	Water
Abaco Beach Resort	Sept 8 to Feb 28	$1.35/ft	$0.65/KWh	$0.15/gal	Mar 1 to Sept 7	$2.25/ft	$0.65/KWh	$0.15/gal
Baker's Bay Club	All Year	$3.00/ft/day						
Berry Islands Club	All Year	$1.00/ft/day	$0.47/KWh	$0.35/gal	Moorings $25/day			
Bimini Bay Resort and Marina	Sept 15 to Apr 15	$1.00/ft/day	$0.60/KWh	$0.45/gal	Apr 16 to Sept 14	$2.00/ft/day	$0.60/KWh	$0.45/gal
Bimini Big Game Marina	Oct 1 to Mar 31	$1.25/ft/day	$15/day+	$0.30/gal	Apr 1 to Sep 30	$1.50/ft/day	$15/day+	$0.30/gal
Bimini Blue Water Resort	All Year	$1.00/ft/day	$10/day+	$0.60/gal				
Bimini Sands Resort & Marina	All Year	$1.10/ft/day	$10/day	$0.35/gal				
Black Sound Marina	All Year	$1.00/ft/day	$15/day	$0.30/gal				
Bluff House Club and Marina	Sep 1 to Mar 31	$0.75/ft/day	$12.50/day	$0.20/gal	Apr 1 to Aug 31	$0.80/ft/day	$12.50/day	$0.20/gal
Boat Harbour Marina	Sep 9 to Feb 28	$1.35/ft/day	$0.65/KWh	$0.15/gal	Mar 1 to Sept 8	$2.25/ft/day	$0.65/KWh	$0.15/gal
Browns Hotel & Marina	All Year	$1.75/ft/day	$20/day+	$.030/gal				
Cat Cay Yacht Club	All Year	$3.25/ft/day	$0.65/KWh	$0.40/gal				
Chub Cay Marina	Jul 25 to Feb 17	$2.75/ft/day	$0.65/KWh	$0.40/gal	Feb 18 to July 24	$4.35/ft/day	$0.65KWh	$0.40/gal
Compass Cay Marina	All Year	$2.50/ft/day	$40/day+	$0.50/gal				
Conch Inn Marina	Sep 1 to Feb 28	$0.70/ft/day	$0.60/KWh	$50/month	Mar 1 to Aug 31	$0.95/ft/day	$0.60/KWh	$50/month
Emerald Bay Marina	All Year	$0.75/ft	$0.85/KWh	$0.40/gal				
Exuma Docking Services	All Year	$1.00/ft/day	$10/day+	$0.20/gal				
Farmers Cay Yacht Club	All Year	$1.50/ft/day+	$15/day+	$0.50/gal	Moorings $10/day			
Grand Bahama Yacht Club	Oct 1 to Feb 28	$1.00/ft/day	$0.45/KWh	$5/day	Mar 1 to Sept 30	$1.30/ft/day	$0.45/KWh	$5/day
Great Harbour Cay Marina	All Year	$1.50/ft/day	$0.75/KWh	$0.50/gal				
Green Turtle Club Marina	See website							
Harbour View Marina	Sep 1 to Feb 28	$0.75/ft/day	$0.60/KWh	$60/month	Mar 1 to Aug 31	$1.00/ft/day	$0.60/KWh	$60/month
Highborne Cay Marina	All Year	$2.10/ft/day+	$25/day+	$0.50/gal				
Hope Town Inn & Marina	All Year	$0.75/ft/day	$0.65/KWh	$0.25/gal				
Hurricane Hole Marina	Call for rates				16 moorings also available @ $20/day.			

Name	Season 1	Month $/ft	Elect 30A	Water	Season 2	Month $/ft	Elect	Water
Lighthouse Marina	All Year	$0.75/ft/day	$10/day+	$0.25/gal	Boat yard.			
Man-O-War Marina	All Year	$1.00/ft/day	$0.50/KWh	$0.25/gal				
Mangoes	Sep 1 to Apr 1	$0.55/ft/day	$0.60/KWh	$60/mo	Apr 1 to Sept 1	$0.75/ft/day	$0.60/KWh	$5/day
Marina at Atlantis	Nov 14 to Aug 15	$4.00/ft/day +	$0.65/KWh	$0.25/gal	Aug 16 to Nov 13	$3.00/ft/day +	$0.65/KWh	$0.25/gal
Marsh Harbour Marina	All year	$0.65/ft/day	$0.60/KWh	$0.50/gal				
Nassau Yacht Haven	Jun 1 to Oct 30	$1.00/ft/day	$0.65/KWh	$8/day				
Nassau Harbour Club	Call for rates.							
Ocean Reef Yacht Club	All Year	$425<42'	$0.50/KWh	Included				
Old Bahama Bay Marina	Sep 7 to Mar 31	$0.90/ft/day	$0.60/KWh	$15/day+	Apr 1 to Sept 16	$1.50/ft/day	$0.55/KWh	$15/day+
Orchid Bay Marina	All Year	$1.25/ft/day	$0.60/KWh	$30/day				
Other Shore Club, The	All Year	$0.80/ft/day	$12/day+	$0.30/gal				
Port Lucaya Marina	All Year	$1.30/ft/day+	$0.45/KWh	$100/mo				
Rosie's Place	All Year	$0.75/ft/day	$10/day+	$0.25/gal				
Sampson Cay Marina	All Year	Call for rate	Metered	$0.50/gal				
Sea Crest Marina	All Year	$1.00/ft/day	$14/day+	$0.30/gal				
Sea Spray Marina	Sept 1 to Mar 31	$1.90/ft/day	$0.65/KWh	$0.40/gal	Jan 1 to Aug 31	$1.35/ft/day	$0.65/KWh	$0.40/gal
Spanish Cay Marina	Sep 15 to Feb 28	$1.00/ft/day	$12/day+	$0.40/gal	Mar 15 to Sep 1	$1.95/ft/day	$20/day+	$0.25/gal
Staniel Cay Yacht Club	All Year	$2.00/ft/day	$0.75/KWh	$0.40/gal				
Treasure Cay Marina	Sept to Mar 31	$0.85/ft/day	$17/day+	$7/day	Apr 1 to Jul 31	$1.50/ft/day	$17/day+	$7/day
Walkers Cay Marina	Call for rates.							
Weech's Bimini Dock	All Year	$0.85/ft/day	$15/day+	NA				
Xanadu Beach Marina	Call for rates.							

Appendix G – Marina Information

Abaco Beach Resort, Boat Harbour, Great Abaco Island   **PH:** 242-367-2158   **FAX:** 242-367-2819
Email/Website: www.abacobeachresort.com   **Harbor:** B   **Town:** 0.2 **Slips:** 192   **Fuel:** Y
Info@abacobeachresort.com   **Washers$** Y   **Cable:** Y   **Internet:** WiFi

Baker's Bay Club, Great Guana Cay, Abaco   **PH:** 272-365-5280   **FAX:** N
Email/Website: www.bakersbayclub.com   **Harbor:** B   **Town:** 0.2 **Slips:** 157   **Fuel:** Y
Info@bakersbayclub.com   **Washers$** Y   **Cable:** N   **Internet:** WiFi

Berry Islands Club, Frazer Hog Cay, Berry Islands   **PH:** 504-655-8464   **FAX:** NA
Email/Website: www.theberryislandsclub.com   **Harbor:** F   **Town:** 4.5 **Slips:** 12   **Fuel:** Y
Info@theberryislandsclub.com   **Washer$** NA   **Cable:** N   **Internet:** WiFi

Bimini Bay Resort and Marina, Bimini Bay, Bimini   **PH:** 242-347-6031   **FAX:** 242-347-2312
Email/Website: www.biminibayresort.com   **Harbor:** D   **Town:** NA **Slips:** 134   **Fuel:** N
marina@biminibayresort.com   **Washer$** NA   **Cable:** N   **Internet:** WiFi

Bimini Big Game Marina, Alice Town, Bimini   **PH:** 242.347.3391   **FAX:** 242.347.3392
Email/Website: www.biggamebimini.com   **Harbor:** D   **Town:** 0.3 **Slips:** 75   **Fuel:** N
sales@fuyharveyoutpost.com   **Washer$** NA   **Cable:** Y   **Internet:** WiFi

Bimini Blue Water Resort, Alice Town, Bimini   **PH:** 242-347-3166   **FAX:** 242-347-3293
Email/Website: NA   **Harbor:** D   **Town:** 0.2 **Slips:** 32   **Fuel:** Y
   Washer$ NA   **Cable:** N   **Internet:** WiFi

Bimini Sands Resort & Marina, Alice Town, Bimini   **PH:** 242.347.3500   **FAX:** 242.347.3501
Email/Website: www.biminisands.com   **Harbor:** A   **Town:** 1   **Slips:** 22   **Fuel:** Y
Info @biminisands.com   **Washer$** 3.00   **Cable:** N   **Internet:** WiFi

Black Sound Marina, Green Turtle Cay, Abacos   **PH:** 242-365-4531   **FAX:** 242-365-4567
Email/Website: NA   **Harbor:** A   **Town:** 0.5 **Slips:** 15   **Fuel:** N
   Washer$: 8.00   **Cable:** N   **Internet:** N

Bluff House Club & Marina, Green Turtle Cay, Abacos   **PH:** 242.365.4247   **FAX:** 242.365.4248
Email/Website: www.bluffhouse.com   **Harbor:** A   **Town:** 3   **Slips:** 40   **Fuel:** Y
   Washer $: 4.00   **Cable:** N   **Internet:** Office

Boat Harbour Marina, Marsh Harbour, Abacos   **PH:** 242.367.2158   **FAX:** 242.367.2819
Email/Website: www,abacobeachresort.com   **Harbor:** A   **Town:** 1   **Slips:** 200   **Fuel:** Y
   Washer$: unk   **Cable:** Y   **Internet:** WiFi

Browns Hotel & Marina, Alice Town, Bimini   **PH:** 305-423-3213 US **FAX:** 305-423-3205US
Email/Website: www.brownshotelandmarina.com   **Harbor:** A   **Town:** 1   **Slips:** 50   **Fuel:** N
Info@bigjohnshotel.com   **Washer$** Y   **Cable:** Y   **Internet:** N

Cat Cay Yacht Club, Cat Cay   **PH:** 242-347-3565   **FAX:** 242-347-3564
Email/Website: www.catcayyachtclub.com   **Harbor:** B   **Town:** NA **Slips:** 107   **Fuel:** Y
   Washer$: 1.00   **Cable:** Y   **Internet:** WiFi

Chub Cay Marina, Chub Cay, Berry Islands   **PH:** 242.325.1490   **FAX:** 242.325.7086
Email/Website: www.chubcay.com   **Harbor:** A   **Town:** NA **Slips:** 110   **Fuel:** Y
     Washer$: 3.00   **Cable:** N   **Internet:** N

Compass Cay Marina, Compass Cay, Exumas   **PH:** 242-355-2137   **FAX:** 242-355-2064
Email/Website: www.compasscay.com   **Harbor:** B   **Town:** NA **Slips:** 12   **Fuel:** N
     compasscay@aol.com   **Washer$:** 5.00   **Cable:** N   **Internet:** WiFi

Conch Inn Marina, Marsh Harbour, Abacos   **PH:** 242.367.4000   **FAX:** 242.367.4004
Email/Website: www.conchinn.com   **Harbor:** B   **Town:** 0.5 **Slips:** 80   **Fuel:** Y
     themoorings@batelnet.bs   **Washer$:** 12.00   **Cable:** Y   **Internet:** WiFi

Emerald Bay Marina, Farmers Hill, Great Exuma   **PH:** 242-336-6100   **FAX:** 242- 336-6101
Email/Website: www.emeraldbayresort.com   **Harbor:** A   **Town:** 2.0 **Slips:** 190   **Fuel:** Y
     Washer$ Y   **Cable:** Y   **Internet:** WiFi

Exuma Docking Services, George Town, Great Exuma   **PH:** 242-336-2578   **FAX:** 242-336-2023
Email/Website: exumadocking@yahoo.com   **Harbor:** C   **Town:** 0.1 **Slips:** 52   **Fuel:** Y
     Washer$: 1.50   **Cable:** N   **Internet:** WiFi

Farmers Cay Yacht Club, Little Farmers Cay, Exumas   **PH:** 242-355-4017   **FAX:** 242-355-4030
Email/Website: **Harbor:** D   **Town:** 0.5 **Slips:** 5   **Fuel:** N
     Washer$: 4   **Cable:** N   **Internet:** WiFi

Grand Bahama Yacht Club, Freeport, Grand Bahama   **PH: 242-373-7616**   **FAX:** 242-373-7630
Email/Website: www.grandbahamayachtclub.com   **Harbor:** A   **Town:** 4   **Slips:** 125   **Fuel:** Y
     info@grandbahamayc.com   **Washer$** 1.25   **Cable:** Y   **Internet:** WiFi

Great Harbour Cay Marina, Great Harbour Cay, Berry Is   **PH:** 242-367-8005   **FAX:** 242-367-8115
Email/Website: info@greatharbourmarina.com   **Harbor:** A   **Town:** 2   **Slips:** 80   **Fuel:** Y
     Washer$ 2.50   **Cable:** N   **Internet:** N

Green Turtle Club Marina, Green Turtle Cay, Abacos   **PH:** 242.365.4271   **FAX:** 242.365.4272
Email/Website: www.greenturtleclub.com   **Harbor:** A   **Town:** 2   **Slips:** 40   **Fuel:** Y
     info@greenturtleclub.com   **Washer$:** 4.25   **Cable:** Y   **Internet:** WiFi

Happy People Marina, Staniel Cay, Exumas   **PH:** 242-355-2008   **FAX:** 242-355-2025
Email/Website: NA   **Harbor:** D   **Town:** 4   **Slips:** 7   **Fuel:** N
     Closed   **Washer$:** NA   **Cable:** N   **Internet:** N

Harbour View Marina, Marsh Harbour, Abacos   **PH:** 242.367.3910   **FAX:** 242.367.3911
Email/Website: www.harbourviewmarina.com   **Harbor:** B   **Town:** 0.2 **Slips:** 40   **Fuel:** Y
     info@harbourviewmarina.com   **Washer$:** 4.00   **Cable:** Y   **Internet:** Y

Highbourne Cay Marina, Highbourne Cay, Exumas   **PH:** 242-355-1008   **FAX:** 242-355-1003
Email/Website: NA   **Harbor:** B   **Town:** NA **Slips:** 25   **Fuel:** Y
     Washer$: 10.00   **Cable:** N   **Internet:** WiFi

Hope Town Inn and Marina, Elbow Cay, Abacos   PH: 242.366.0003   FAX: 242.366.0254
Email/Website: www.clubsoleil.com   **Harbor: A**   **Town:** 0.2 **Slips:** 16   **Fuel: N**
info@clubsoleil.com   **Washer$:** 4.00   **Cable: N**   **Internet:** WiFi

Hurricane Hole Marina, Nassau, Paradise Island   PH: 242-363-3600   FAX: 242-363-3604
Email/Website: www.hurricaneholemarina.com   **Harbor: A**   **Town:** 0.5 **Slips:** 90   **Fuel: Y**
info@hurricaneholemarina.com   **Washer$:** 3.00   **Cable: Y**   **Internet: N**

Lighthouse Marina, Elbow Cay, Abacos   PH: 242.366.0154   FAX: 242.366.0171
Email/Website: www.lighthousemarina.com   **Harbor: A**   **Town:** 0.2 **Slips:** 5   **Fuel: Y**
info@htlighthousemarina.com   **Washers$:** 4.00   **Cable: N**   **Internet: N**

Man O War Marina, Man-O-War Cay, Abacos   PH: 242.365.6008   FAX: 242.365.6151
Email/Website: www.manowarmarina.com   **Harbor: A**   **Town:** 0   **Slips:** 26   **Fuel: Y**
info@manowarmarina.com   **Washer$: 3.50**   **Cable: Y**   **Internet:** WiFi

Mangoes Marina, Marsh Harbour, Abacos   PH: 242.367.2366   **FAX:** None
Email/Website: www.mangoesmarina.com   **Harbor: B**   **Town:** 0.3 **Slips:** 31   **Fuel: N**
John-mangoes@gmail.com   **Washer$:** 3.50   **Cable: Y**   **Internet: Y**

Marina at Atlantis, Nassau, Paradise Island   PH: 242-363-6068   FAX: 242-363-6008
Email/Website: www.atlantis.com   **Harbor: A**   **Town:** 1   **Slips:** 63   **Fuel: N**
Washer$: 2.00   **Cable: N**   **Internet: N**

Marsh Harbour Marina, Marsh Harbour, Abacos   PH: 242-367-2700   FAX: 242-367-2033
Email/Website: www.jibroom.com   **Harbor: B**   **Town:** 1.5 **Slips:** 68   **Fuel: Y**
JibRoom@hotmail.com   **Washer$:** 3.00   **Cable: Y**   **Internet: Y**

Nassau Harbour Club, Nassau, New Providence   PH: 242-393-0771   FAX: 242-393-5393
Email/Website: NA   **Harbor: C**   **Town:** 0.5 **Slips:** 65   **Fuel: Y**
Washer$: 3.00   **Cable: N**   **Internet:** WiFi

Nassau Yacht Haven, Nassau, New Providence   PH: 242-393-8173   FAX: 242-393-3429
Email/Website: www.nassauyachthaven.com   **Harbor: C**   **Town:** 0.4 **Slips:** 120   **Fuel: N**
info@nassauyachthaven.com   **Washer$** 2.00   **Cable: N**   **Internet:** WiFi

Ocean Reef Yacht Club, Freeport, Grand Bahama Is   PH: 242.373.4661   FAX: 242.373.8261
Email/Website: www.oryc.com   **Harbor: A**   **Town:**   **Slips:** 50   **Fuel: N**
edawkinsoryc@coralwave.com   **Washers$:** Unk   **Cable: Y**   **Internet:** WiFi

Old Bahama Bay Marina, West End, Grand Bahama Is   PH: 242.350.6500   FAX: 242.350.6565
Email/Website: www.oldbahamabay.com   **Harbor: A**   **Town:** 25 **Slips:** 72   **Fuel: Y**
Washer$: 2.00   **Cable: Y**   **Internet: Y**

Orchid Bay Marina, Great Guana Cay, Abacos   PH: 242.365.5175   FAX: 242.365.5166
Email/Website: www.orchidbay.net   **Harbor: B**   **Town:** .06 **Slips:** 66   **Fuel: Y**
Washer$: 5.00   **Cable: N**   **Internet:** WiFi

Other Shore Club, The, Green Turtle Cay, Abacos   **PH:** 242.365.4226   **FAX:** NA
     Email/Website: www.othershoreclub.com   **Harbor:** A   **Town:** 0.6 **Slips:** 15   **Fuel:** N
                                  Washer$: NA   **Cable:** N   **Internet:** WiFi

Port Lucaya Marina, Freeport, Grand Bahama Is   **PH:** 242.373.9090   **FAX:** 242.373.8632
     Email/Website: www.portlucayamarina.com   **Harbor:** A   **Town:** 3   **Slips:** 100   **Fuel:** Y
           info@portlucayamarina.com   **Washer$:** Unk   **Cable:** Y   **Internet:** Y

Rosies Place, Grand Cay, Abacos   **PH:** 242-727-4477   **FAX:** NA
     Email/Website: www.rosiesplace.com   **Harbor:** C   **Town:** 0.1 **Slips:** 15   **Fuel:** Y
           motel@rosiesplace.com   **Washer$:** 3.00   **Cable:** N   **Internet:** N

Sampson Cay Marina, Samson Cay, Exumas   **PH:** 242.355.2034   **FAX:** 242.357.0824
     Email/Website: www.sampsoncayclub.com   **Harbor:** A   **Town:** NA **Slips:** 30   **Fuel:** Y
           food@sampsoncayclub.com   **Washer$:** 4.00   **Cable:** N   **Internet:** WiFi

Sea Crest Marina, Alice Town, Bimini   **PH:** 242.347.3071   **FAX:** 242.347.3495
     Email/Website: www.seacrestbimini.com   **Harbor:** D   **Town:** 0.1 **Slips:** 14   **Fuel:** N
                                  Washer$: NA   **Cable:** N   **Internet:** WiFi

Sea Spray Marina, White Sound, Elbow Cay, Abacos   **PH:** 242.366.0065   **FAX:** 242.366.0383
     Email/Website: www.seasprayresort.com   **Harbor:** B   **Town:** 3   **Slips:** 60   **Fuel:** Y
           info@seasprayresort.com   **Washer$:** 15/load **Cable:** N   **Internet:** WiFi

Spanish Cay Marina, Spanish Cay, Abacos   **PH:** 242.365.0083   **FAX:** 242.365.0453
     Email/Website: www.spanishcay.com   **Harbor:** B   **Town:** NA **Slips:** 81   **Fuel:** Y
           spanishcay@aol.com   **Washer$:** Y   **Cable:** N   **Internet:** WiFi

Staniel Cay Yacht Club, Staniel Cay, Exumas   **PH:** 242.355.2024   **FAX:** 242.355.2044
     Email/Website: www.stanielcay.com   **Harbor:** D   **Town:** 0.3 **Slips:** 18   **Fuel:** Y
           info@stanielcay.com   **Washer$:** 10.00   **Cable:** N   **Internet:** WiFi

Treasure Cay Marina, Treasure Cay, Abacos   **PH:** 242.365.8250   **FAX:** 242.365.8362
     Email/Website: www.treasurecay.com   **Harbor:** A   **Town:** 0.2 **Slips:** 150   **Fuel:** Y
           info@treasurecay.com   **Washer$:** 2.75   **Cable:** Y   **Internet:** WiFi

Walker's Cay Marina, Walker's Cay, Abacos   **PH:** 242-353-1252   **FAX:** NA
     Email/Website: www.walkerscay.com   **Harbor:** A   **Town:** NA **Slips:** 40   **Fuel:** Y
           info@walkerscay.com   **Washer$:**   **Cable:** N   **Internet:** N

Weech's Bimini Dock, Alice Town, Bimini   **PH:** 242-347-3028   **FAX:** 242-347-3508
     Email/Website: www.weechsbiminidock.com   **Harbor:** D   **Town:** 0.2 **Slips:** 15   **Fuel:** N
                                  Washer$: NA   **Cable:** N   **Internet:** N

Xanadu Beach Marina, Freeport, Grand Bahama Is   **PH:** 242-352-6782   **FAX:** 242-352-5799
     Email/Website: www.xanadubeachhotel.com   **Harbor:** A   **Town:** 5   **Slips:** 60   **Fuel:** Y
           info@xanadubeachhotel.com   **Washer$:** NA   **Cable:** N   **Internet:** N

Appendix H

Many thanks to the individuals listed below who provided updates to this and previous editions of the Bahamas Bound book.

Alan and Susann Syme	*Kaos*
Bill Hezlep	*Walkabout*
Bob Wilkins	*True Grit*
Chuck Baier and Susan Landry	*Beach House*
Bud and Elaine Lloyd	*Diamond Girl*
Dave McGuire	
Doreen Duffy	*Puca*
Ellen and Floyd	*Spirit*
Guy Goodwin	
Harold and Dee Rudd	*Lady Dee*
Ian and Sue Lemair	*Kokopelli*
Jack Dozier	*Waterway Guide Lady*
Janice Callum	*Calamus*
Jerry and Dale Mann	*Wanderer*
Jim and Kay Stolte	*Siris IV*
Jim Booth	
Joe and Candi Nilles	*Ja-C-Jo*
Judy and John Gill	*Two J's V*
Lee and Kay Ladd	*DBL-ELL*
Leo and Mona Oxberger	*Snug*
Rick Butler	
Robert Wilson	*Sea Island Girl*
Rosalie and Robert Beasley	*Rosalie Ann*
Sue and Paul Graham	*Odyssey*

Note: Significant changes to the information in this publication will be posted on the Skipper Bob website, www.skipperbob.net, and incorporated into the next edition.

Abaco Map - 56
Abaco Yacht Services - 59
Abacos – 10,52
Alice Town - 63
Allen's Cay - 67
Allans-Pensacola Cay - 55
AM/FM radio - 24
Anchoring - 20
Anchors - 20
Andros - 12
Appendix A - 75
Appendix B – 76
Appendix C - 78
Appendix D – 80
Appendix E - 81
Appendix F - 83
Appendix G - 85
Appendix H - 89
Approaches to Abaco - 52
Atlantis - 67
ATM - 44
Bahamas cruising fee - 41
Bahamas geography - 2
Bahamas independence - 7
Bahamas time - 42
Bahamas VHF license - 24
Bahamian Coast Guard - 40
Bahamian money - 44
Bahamian mooring - 21
Bananas - 45
Bank hours - 44
BASRA - 40
Bayshore Marine - 65
Beer - 28
Bell Island - 69
Berry Islaland Club - 64
Berry Islands – 12, 63
Bicycles - 50
Big Grand Cay - 55
Bimini - 63
Bimini Big Game Marina - 63

Bimini Blue Water Resort - 63
Bimini Sands - 63
Bitter Guana Cay - 70
Black Point - 71
Black Sound Marina - 57
Bluff House Marina - 57
Boat Harbour Marina - 59
Browns Marina - 63
BTC - 48
Buddy boat - 35
Camp Driftwood - 68
Canned meat - 28
Capt Sayle - 6
Caribbean Marine Research - 72
Carters Cay - 55
Cat Cay - 63
Cat Cay Yacht Club - 63
Cellular phones - 48
Channel markers - 42
Chapter 1 - 1
Chapter 2 - 8
Chapter 3 - 15
Chapter 4 - 31
Chapter 5 - 42
Chapter 6 - 52
Chapter 7 - 62
Charcoal filter - 25
Chart book – 32,75
Charts - 27
Chlorine - 25
Chub Cay - 64
Chub Cay Marina - 64
Cigarettes - 27
Clearing customs - 40
CMG - 33
COG - 33
Coldfronts – 9, 37
Columbus - 6
Compass Cay - 69
Compass Cay Marina - 70
Conch Cay Cut - 73

Conch Cut – 69
Conch Inn Marina - 59
Contributors - 89
Coopers Town - 56
Copy of registration - 17
Coral heads - 8
Courtesy flag - 16
Credit cards - 44
Crossing table - 34
Crossing, the - 31
Cruiser's Net - 50
Cruising fee - 15,41
Cruising guides - 27
Cruising permit – 15, 41
Cruising stores - 78
Customs and food - 29
Customs decal - 15
Customs documentation - 40
Departing Nassau - 66
Departure time - 38
Dinghy - 18
Direct TV - 23
Dish - 23
Diving - 23
Documentation - 17
Double Breasted Cay - 55
Drinking water - 25
DT - 15
Duty Tax - 15
Eating out – 28, 45
Elbow Cay - 60
Eleuthera – 6, 12
Elizabeth Harbour - 73
E-Mail - 48
Emerald Bay Marina - 72
Exchange rate - 44
Exuma Docking Services - 73
Exumas – 11, 62
Exumas map - 65
Farmer's Cay Yacht Club - 71
FCC fee - 24

Bahamas Bound
Index